Mosaic Magic
Afghans Made Easy

by Lily M. Chin

Oxmoor
House®

Mosaic Magic: Afghans Made Easy

Published by Oxmoor House, Inc., and Leisure Arts, Inc.

Library of Congress Catalog Card Number: 99-75769
Hardcover ISBN: 0-8487-1902-6
Softcover ISBN: 0-8487-1903-4
Printed in the United States of America
First Printing 1999

Editor-in-Chief: Nancy Fitzpatrick Wyatt
Senior Crafts Editor: Susan Ramey Cleveland
Senior Editor, Copy and Homes: Olivia Kindig Wells
Art Director: James Boone

Mosaic Magic: Afghans Made Easy

Contributing Editor: Janica York
Copy Editor: L. Amanda Owens
Contributing Copy Editor: Margaret Allen Price
Associate Art Director: Cynthia R. Cooper
Senior Designer: Larry Hunter
Contributing Designer: Carol Damsky
Contributing Illustrators: Barbara Ball, Anita Bice
Senior Photographer: John O'Hagan
Photo Stylist: Linda Baltzell Wright
Director, Production and Distribution: Phillip Lee
Associate Production Manager: Theresa L. Beste
Production Assistant: Faye Porter Bonner
Publishing Systems Administrator: Rick Tucker

We're Here for You!

We at Oxmoor House are dedicated to serving you with
reliable information that expands your imagination and
enriches your life. We welcome your comments and
suggestions. Please write us at:

Oxmoor House, Inc.
Editor, *Mosaic Magic: Afghans Made Easy*
2100 Lakeshore Drive
Birmingham, AL 35209

To order additional publications, call 1-205-877-6560.

Table of Contents

Page 52

Page 16

Kind Crocheters,

Have you ever yearned for a simple-to-do project that looks deceptively complex? I relish an easy technique that yields intricate-looking results. The patterns I developed in **Mosaic Magic: Afghans Made Easy** are all based on this idea of creating a colorful end product with very little effort.

Knitters have been using such a mosaic technique for years, and I decided it was time for crocheters to benefit from this concept, which emulates the lush color patterns reminiscent of inlaid tiles.

Mosaic crochet starts with rows of simple single crochet stitches. In fact, you only work with one color on a row at a time, so you don't have to worry about constantly changing colors within a row. This avoids tangled skeins, loose ends that must be woven in later, and lots of frustration!

The seeming complexity comes from "dropping" long double crochet stitches from the working row to another row below. Dropping stitches of one color into another creates the interlocking color patterns unique to mosaic crochet. You can drop stitches vertically or diagonally and combine them to make V-stitches and X-stitches. You will be surprised at the terrific texture you also get by dropping stitches without switching colors. Add post stitches to the mix for even more texture.

If you're like me, you enjoy both the process and the product of crochet. I know you'll like this new process, and I want you to love the end results as well. So I've included a broad range of cozy and colorful afghans to fit a host of decors.

As an added benefit, I list stitch multiples in the gauge instructions. For those of you who aren't familiar with multiples, they are the number of stitches required to create a specified stitch pattern. Use these easy formulas to develop your own projects—not just afghans, but scarves, stoles, and other garments.

Lion Brand Yarn Company generously provided a variety of yarns in a multitude of hues and textures for the projects photographed in this book. I enjoyed experimenting with the different blends, including mohair, rayon, wool, chenille, and alpaca.

I hope you will find mosaic crochet as versatile and as fun as I do. My wish is to inspire you to use the patterns and the techniques presented here to spur your own creative ideas and uses.

Enjoy,

Lily McCai

This book is for my mom, Linda Chin, who got me started on crochet, and for my husband, Clifford Pearson, who held my hand every step of the way.

Bargello

Combine cream and coffee for a rich-looking throw that imitates seventeenth-century bargello embroidery. Finish it with a unique border by using two strands of yarn at once.

Materials

Sportweight acrylic micro-fiber yarn, approximately:
25 oz. (1,680 yd.) cream, MC
25 oz. (1,680 yd.) tan, CC
Size H crochet hook or size to obtain gauge

Finished Size

Approximately 47" x 55"

Gauge

In pat, 14 sts and 18 rows = 4"

Gauge Swatch *(Multiple of 12 sts + 8)*

With CC, ch 32. Work in pat for 20 rows.

Pattern Stitch

Long double crochet [Ldc]: Yo, insert hook from front to back in st indicated, yo and pull up long lp, (yo and pull through 2 lps) twice.

Note: To change colors, work last yo of prev st with new color, dropping prev color to ws of work. Do not fasten off when changing colors.

With CC, ch 164 loosely.

Row 1 (ws): Sc in 2nd ch from hook and in ea ch across, change to MC in last st: 163 sc.

Row 2 (rs): With MC, ch 1, turn; sc in first sc and in ea sc across.

Row 3: Ch 1, turn; sc in first sc and in ea st across, change to CC in last st.

Row 4: With CC, ch 1, turn; sc in first sc, Ldc in 2nd st from beg 3 rows below, * (sk next sc on working row, sc in next sc, Ldc in 2nd st from prev Ldc 3 rows below) twice, sk next sc on working row **, sc in next 2 sc, Ldc in 4th sc from prev Ldc 3 rows below, sk next sc on working row, sc in next sc, Ldc in same sc as prev Ldc 3 rows below [V-st made], sk next sc on working row, sc in next 2 sc, Ldc in 4th sc from prev Ldc 3 rows below; rep from * across, ending last rep at **, sc in last sc: 42 Ldc and 13 V-sts.

Row 5: Ch 1, turn; sc in first sc and in ea st across, change to MC in last st.

Row 6: With MC, ch 1, turn; sc in first 2 sc, Ldc in 3rd st from beg 3 rows below, * sk next sc on working row, sc in next sc, Ldc in 2nd st from prev Ldc 3 rows below, sk next sc on working row **, sc in next 3 sc, Ldc in 5th sc from prev Ldc 3 rows below, sk next sc on working row, sc in next sc, Ldc in same sc as prev Ldc 3 rows below [V-st made], sk next sc on working row, sc in next 3 sc, Ldc in 5th sc from prev Ldc 3 rows below; rep from * across, ending last rep at **, sc in last 2 sc: 28 Ldc and 13 V-sts.

Rows 7–244: Rep rows 3–6, 59 times, then rep rows 3 and 4 once; do not turn after last row; fasten off MC; do not fasten off CC.

Border

Rnd 1 (rs): With rs facing and CC, ch 1, 3 sc in last st, work 187 sc evenly across to next corner, 3 sc in corner, sc in ea ch across to next corner [161 sc], 3 sc in corner, work 187 sc evenly across to next corner, 3 sc in corner, sc in ea st across to next corner [161 sc], change to MC in last st; join with sl st to beg sc: 708 sc.

Rnd 2 (ws): Ch 1, turn; * sc in ea sc across to corner, 3 sc in corner; rep from * around, change to CC in last st; join with sl st to beg sc: 716 sc.

Rnd 3 (rs): With CC, ch 1, turn; sc in first sc, ch 3, drop CC lp from hook in front of work, pick up MC, sl st in next sc, ch 1, sc in same sc, * ch 3, drop MC lp from hook, working in front of MC, pick up CC lp **, sc in next sc, ch 3, drop CC lp from hook, working in front of CC, pick up MC lp, sc in next sc; rep from * around, ending last rep at **; join CC with sl st to beg CC sc; fasten off CC; pick up MC lp; join MC with sl st to beg MC sc; fasten off.

Note: Stitches in rnd 3 will twist yarns, so untangle skeins every few stitches.

Project was stitched by Joann Moss with Microspun: French Vanilla #98 and Mocha #124.

Baby Blocks

These delicate shades not only blend with most nursery colors but also make the transition to a young girl's bedroom beautifully.

Materials

Sportweight acrylic yarn, approximately:

5¼ oz. (590 yd.) blue, A
5¼ oz. (590 yd.) green, B
5¼ oz. (590 yd.) lavender, C
5¼ oz. (590 yd.) white, D
5¼ oz. (590 yd.) yellow, E
5¼ oz. (590 yd.) pink, F
Size H crochet hook or size to obtain gauge
Yarn needle

Finished Size

Approximately 41" x 48"

Gauge

Ea Block = 6½"

Gauge Swatch *(Multiple of 4 sts + 2)*

Work as for Block.

Pattern Stitch

Long double crochet [Ldc]: Yo, insert hook from front to back in st indicated, yo and pull up long lp, (yo and pull through 2 lps) twice.

Note: *To change colors, work last yo of prev st with new color, dropping prev color to ws of work. Do not fasten off when changing colors.*

Block Color Combinations:

Number of Blocks	MC	CC
3	A	F
3	B	F
3	C	F
3	F	A
3	F	B
3	F	C
2	A	D
2	B	D
2	C	D
2	D	A
2	D	B
2	D	C
2	A	E
2	B	E
2	C	E
2	E	A
2	E	B
2	E	C

Block *(Make 42.)*

With MC, ch 26 loosely.

Row 1 (ws): Sc in 2nd ch from hook and in ea ch across, change to CC in last st: 25 sc.

Row 2 (rs): With CC, ch 1, turn; sc in first sc and in ea sc across.

Row 3: Ch 1, turn; sc in first sc and in ea st across, change to MC in last st.

Row 4: With MC, ch 1, turn; sc in first sc, Ldc in 4th sc from beg 3 rows below, * sk next sc on working row, sc in next sc, Ldc in 2nd sc before prev Ldc 3 rows below [X-st made], sk next sc on working row, sc in next sc **, Ldc in 4th sc from prev Ldc 3 rows below; rep from * across, ending last rep at **: 6 X-sts.

Row 5: Ch 1, turn; sc in first sc and in ea st across, change to CC in last st.

Row 6: With CC, ch 1, turn; sc in first 3 sc, Ldc in 6th sc from beg 3 rows below, * sk next sc on working row, sc in next sc, Ldc in 2nd sc before prev Ldc 3 rows below [X-st made], sk next sc on working row, sc in next sc **, Ldc in 4th sc from prev Ldc 3 rows below; rep from * across, ending last rep at **, sc in last 2 sc: 5 X-sts.

Rows 7–32: Rep rows 3–6, 6 times, then rep rows 3 and 4 once; fasten off after last row.

Assembly

Afghan is 6 Blocks wide and 7 Blocks long. Arrange Blocks as shown in **Assembly Diagram,** turning every other Block sideways. Whipstitch Blocks tog.

AF	BF	CF	FA	FB	FC
AE	BE	CE	EA	EB	EC
AD	BD	CD	DA	DB	DC
AF	BF	CF	FA	FB	FC
AE	BE	CE	EA	EB	EC
AD	BD	CD	DA	DB	DC
AF	BF	CF	FA	FB	FC

Assembly Diagram

(Continued on page 10)

Border

Rnd 1 (rs): With rs facing, join E in any corner with sl st, ch 1, * sc evenly across to next corner, 3 sc in corner; rep from * around; join with sl st to beg sc; fasten off.

Rnd 2 (ws): With ws facing, join C in any corner with sl st, ch 1, * sc in ea sc across to next corner, 3 sc in corner; rep from * around; join with sl st to beg sc; fasten off.

Rnd 3 (rs): With D, rep rnd 1.
Rnd 4 (ws): With B, rep rnd 2.
Rnd 5 (rs): With F, rep rnd 1.
Rnd 6 (ws): With B, rep rnd 2.

Project was stitched by Peggy Stiver with Jamie Pompadour: Pastel Blue #206, Pastel Green #269, and Lavender #244; and Jamie 3-ply: White #200, Pastel Yellow #257, and Pink #201.

Victorian Elegance

*An abundance of stitch patterns, heirloom colors, and opulent fringe
gives this afghan the appeal of a bygone era.*

Materials

Worsted-weight cotton yarn, approximately:
40 oz. (1,890 yd.) sage, MC
20 oz. (945 yd.) tan, A
15 oz. (710 yd.) rose, B
15 oz. (710 yd.) cream, C
Size I crochet hook or size to obtain gauge

Finished Size

Approximately 52" x 69"

Gauge

In pat, 12 sts and 15 rows = 4"

Gauge Swatch *(Multiple of 4 sts + 2)*

With MC, ch 22. Work in pat for 20 rows.

Pattern Stitch

Long double crochet [Ldc]: Yo, insert hook from front to back in st indicated, yo and pull up long lp, (yo and pull through 2 lps) twice.

Note: Afghan is worked sideways. To change colors, work last yo of prev st with new color, dropping prev color to ws of work. Do not fasten off when changing colors.

With MC, ch 198 loosely.

Row 1 (ws): Sc in 2nd ch from hook and in ea ch across, change to A in last st: 197 sc.

Row 2 (rs): With A, ch 1, turn; sc in first sc and in ea sc across.

Row 3: Ch 1, turn; sc in first sc and in ea st across, change to MC in last st.

Row 4: With MC, ch 1, turn; sc in first 3 sc, Ldc in 2nd sc from beg 3 rows below [slant-st made], * sk next sc on working row **, sc in next 3 sc, Ldc in 4th sc from prev Ldc 3 rows below [slant-st made]; rep from * across, ending

last rep at **, sc in last sc: 49 slant-sts.

Row 5: Ch 1, turn; sc in first sc and in ea st across, change to A in last st.

Row 6: With A, ch 1, turn; sc in first 4 sc, Ldc in 5th sc from beg 3 rows below, * sk next sc on working row, sc in next 3 sc **, Ldc in 4th sc from prev Ldc 3 rows below; rep from * across, ending last rep at **, sc in last sc: 48 Ldc.

Rows 7–44: Rep rows 3–6, 9 times, then rep rows 3 and 4 once; fasten off A.

Row 45: Ch 1, turn; sc in first sc and in ea st across, change to B in last st.

Rows 46 and 47: With B, rep rows 2 and 3 once.

Row 48: With MC, ch 1, turn; sc in first sc, Ldc in 4th sc from beg 3 rows below [slant-st made], * sk next sc on working row, sc in next 3 sc **, Ldc in 4th sc from prev Ldc [slant-st made]; rep from * across, ending last rep at **: 49 slant-sts.

Row 49: Rep row 45.

Row 50: With B, rep row 6.

Rows 51–53: Rep rows 3–5 once, change to C in last st of last row; fasten off B.

Rows 54 and 55: With C, rep rows 2 and 3 once.

Row 56: Rep row 48.

Row 57: Ch 1, turn; sc in first sc and in ea st across, change to C in last st.

Row 58: With C, rep row 6.

Rows 59–61: Rep rows 3–5 once, change to B in last st of last row; fasten off C.

Rows 62–149: Rep rows 46–61, 5 times, then rep rows 46–53 once, change to A in last st of last row.

Rows 150 and 151: Rep rows 2 and 3 once.

Row 152: Rep row 48.

Rows 153–155: Rep rows 5 and 6 once, then rep row 3 once.

Rows 156–192: Rep rows 152–155, 9 times, then rep row 152 once; do not turn after last row; fasten off MC; do not fasten off A.

Border

With rs facing and A, sl st in top right corner, ch 1, 3 sc in last st, sc in ea st across to next corner, 3 sc in corner, sc evenly across to next corner, 3 sc in corner, sc in ea ch across to next corner, 3 sc in corner, sc evenly across to next corner; join with sl st to beg sc; fasten off.

Note: *Beg working in rows along short edges of afghan.*

Top Edging

Row 1 (ws): With ws facing, join C in top left corner with sl st, ch 1, sc in same sc, * working across short edge of afghan, ch 10, sc in next 2 sc; rep from * across.

Row 2 (rs): Ch 1, turn; keeping ch-10 lps in front of work, sc in first sc and in ea sc across, change to B in last st; fasten off C.

Row 3: Ch 1, turn; sc in first sc, * ch 10, sc in next 2 sc; rep from * across.

Row 4: Ch 1, turn; keeping ch-10 lps in front of work, sc in first sc and in ea sc across, change to MC in last st; fasten off B.

Rows 5 and 6: Rep rows 3 and 4 once; do not change colors in last st of last row; fasten off MC.

Bottom Edging

Row 1 (ws): With ws facing, join C in bottom right corner with sl st, ch 1, sc in same sc, * working across short edge of afghan, ch 10, sc in next 2 sc; rep from * across.

Rows 2–6: Rep rows 2–6 of Top Edging once.

Project was stitched by Peggy Stiver with Kitchen Cotton: Sage #181, Khaki #124, Rose #140, and Natural #98.

Seafoam Stripes

Use fluffy yarn in ocean colors to capture the gentle comfort of the rolling sea.

Materials
Chunky-weight brushed
   acrylic yarn, approximately:
33 oz. (1,485 yd.) cream, MC
Chunky-weight acrylic bouclé
   yarn, approximately:
24 oz. (740 yd.) green, CC
Size K crochet hook or size to
   obtain gauge

Finished Size
Approximately 48" x 63"

Gauge
In pat, 7 sts and 8 rows = 3"

Gauge Swatch *(Multiple of 14 sts + 10)*
With CC, ch 24. Work in pat for
16 rows.

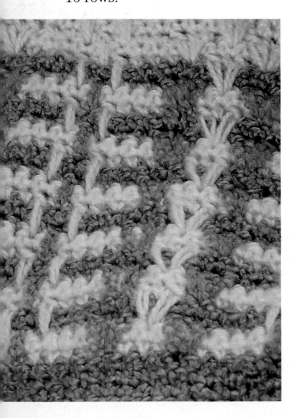

Pattern Stitch
Long double crochet [Ldc]: Yo,
insert hook from front to back in
st indicated, yo and pull up long
lp, (yo and pull through 2 lps)
twice.

*Note: To change colors, work
last yo of prev st with new color,
dropping prev color to ws of
work. Do not fasten off when
changing colors.*

*Color sequence: 1 row CC,
(2 rows MC, 2 rows CC) 6 times,
fasten off CC, * 18 rows MC,
2 rows CC, 2 rows MC, 2 rows
CC, fasten off CC; rep from * 3
times, 18 rows MC, (2 rows CC,
2 rows MC) 6 times, 1 row CC.*

With CC, ch 108 loosely.
Row 1 (ws): Sc in 2nd ch from
hook and in ea ch across: 107 sc.
Row 2 (rs): Ch 1, turn; sc in first
sc and in ea sc across.
Row 3 and all Odd Rows: Ch 1,
turn; sc in first sc and in ea st
across.
Row 4: Ch 1, turn; sc in first sc,
Ldc in 3rd sc from beg 3 rows
below, * sk next sc on working row,
sc in next sc, Ldc in same sc as
prev Ldc 3 rows below [V-st made],
sk next sc on working row, sc in
next sc, Ldc in 4th sc from prev
Ldc 3 rows below, sk next sc on
working row, sc in next sc, Ldc in
same sc as prev Ldc 3 rows below
[V-st made], sk next sc on working
row **, sc in next 3 sc, Ldc in 5th
sc from prev Ldc 3 rows below,
sk next sc on working row, sc in
next 3 sc, Ldc in 5th sc from prev
Ldc 3 rows below; rep from *

across, ending last rep at **, sc in
last sc: 16 V-sts and 7 Ldc.
Row 6: Ch 1, turn; sc in first 3 sc,
Ldc in 5th sc from beg 3 rows
below, * sk next sc on working
row, sc in next sc, Ldc in same sc
as prev Ldc 3 rows below [V-st
made], sk next sc on working
row **, sc in next 4 sc, Ldc in 6th
sc from prev Ldc 3 rows below,
sk next sc on working row, sc in
next sc, Ldc in 2nd sc from prev
Ldc 3 rows below, sk next sc on
working row, sc in next 4 sc,
Ldc in 6th sc from prev Ldc 3
rows below; rep from * across,
ending last rep at **, sc in last 3
sc: 8 V-sts and 14 Ldc.
Rows 7–164: Rep rows 3–6, 39
times, then rep rows 3 and 4
once; fasten off after last row.

Border
Rnd 1 (rs): With rs facing, join
CC in top right corner with sl st,
ch 1, 3 sc in corner, sc in ea st
across to next corner, 3 sc in
corner, sc evenly across to next
corner, 3 sc in corner, sc in ea
ch across to next corner, 3 sc in
corner, sc evenly across to next
corner; join with sl st to beg sc.
Rnd 2 (ws): Ch 1, turn; * sc in
ea sc across to next corner, 3 sc
in corner; rep from * around; join
with sl st to beg sc.
Rnd 3 (rs): Turn; sl st in same sc
and in ea sc around; join with sl
st to beg sl st; fasten off.

*Project was stitched by Joann Moss
with Jiffy: Fisherman #99 and
Homespun: Seaspray #123.*

Spring Flowers

This intricate-looking pattern of tiny flowers is simply a combination of slanted stitches. The Easter-inspired colors create subtle stripes on a robin's egg blue background.

Materials

Worsted-weight mohair-blend yarn, approximately:
15 oz. (1,335 yd.) aqua, MC
12½ oz. (1,110 yd.) white, A
5 oz. (445 yd.) gold, B
2½ oz. (225 yd.) pink, C
Size K crochet hook or size to obtain gauge

Finished Size

Approximately 51" x 56"

Gauge

In pat, 10 sts and 14 rows = 4"

Gauge Swatch *(Multiple of 12 sts + 6)*

With A, ch 18. Work in pat for 18 rows.

Pattern Stitch

Long double crochet [Ldc]: Yo, insert hook from front to back in st indicated, yo and pull up long lp, (yo and pull through 2 lps) twice.

Note: To change colors, work last yo of prev st with new color, dropping prev color to ws of work. Do not fasten off when changing colors.

Color sequence: 1 row A, (2 rows MC, 2 rows A) 5 times, fasten off A, (2 rows MC, 2 rows B) 3 times, 2 rows MC, 2 rows C, fasten off C, (2 rows MC, 2 rows B) 3 times, fasten off B, (2 rows MC, 2 rows A) 24 times, fasten off A, (2 rows MC, 2 rows B) 3 times, 2 rows MC, 2 rows C, fasten off C, (2 rows MC, 2 rows B) 3 times, fasten off B, (2 rows MC, 2 rows A) 4 times, 2 rows MC, 1 row A.

With A, ch 126 loosely.
Row 1 (ws): Sc in 2nd ch from hook and in ea ch across: 125 sc.
Row 2 (rs): Ch 1, turn; sc in first sc and in ea sc across.

Row 3 and all Odd Rows: Ch 1, turn; sc in first sc and in ea st across.

Row 4: Ch 1, turn; sc in first sc, Ldc in 4th sc from beg 3 rows below, * sk next sc on working row, sc in next sc, Ldc in 2nd sc before prev Ldc 3 rows below [X-st made], sk next sc on working row, sc in next sc **, Ldc in 4th sc from prev Ldc 3 rows

(Continued on page 18)

~ 17 ~

below [slant-st made], sk next sc on working row, Ldc in same sc as prev Ldc 3 rows below, sk next sc on working row, sc in next sc, Ldc in 2nd sc from prev Ldc 3 rows below, sk next sc on working row, sc in next sc, Ldc in same sc as prev Ldc 3 rows below [slant-st made], sk next sc on working row, sc in next sc, Ldc in 6th sc from prev Ldc 3 rows below; rep from * across, ending last rep at **: 11 X-sts, 20 slant-sts, and 20 Ldc.

Row 6: Ch 1, turn; sc in first 2 sc, Ldc in 3rd sc from beg 3 rows below, * sk next sc on working row, sc in next sc **, Ldc in 2nd sc from prev Ldc 3 rows below; rep from * across, ending last rep at **; sc in last sc: 61 Ldc.

Rows 7–192: Rep rows 3–6, 46 times, then rep rows 3 and 4

once; do not turn after last row; fasten off MC; do not fasten off A.

Border

Rnd 1 (rs): With rs facing and A, ch 1, 3 sc in last st, work 143 sc evenly across to next corner, 3 sc in corner, sc in ea ch across to next corner, 3 sc in corner, work 143 sc evenly across to next corner, 3 sc in corner, sc in ea st across to next corner; join with sl st to beg sc; fasten off: 544 sc.

Rnd 2 (ws): With ws facing, join B in any corner with sl st, ch 1, * sc in ea sc across to next corner, 3 sc in corner; rep from * around; join with sl st to beg sc; do not fasten off; drop lp from hook: 552 sc.

Rnd 3 (rs): With rs facing, join C in same corner with sl st, ch 5 [counts as dc plus 2 ch], * sk next

sc, dc in next sc, ch 2; rep from * around; join with sl st to 3rd ch of beg ch-5; fasten off C: 276 dc.

Rnd 4 (rs): With rs facing and keeping yarn in back of work, pick up dropped B lp through ch-2 sp, * working around rnd 3 sts, ch 2, drop lp from hook, insert hook in next sk sc on rnd 2, pick up dropped lp and pull lp through sc; rep from * around, ch 1; join with sl st to beg sl st; fasten off.

Project was stitched by Margarete Dahlke with Imagine: Aqua #102, White #100, Maize #186, and Pink #101.

Jumbo Granny Square

A granny square is a great pattern for beginners.
Build this one into a full-size blanket. Then add borders with
a square design that emulates the center panel.

Materials
Worsted-weight wool-blend
yarn, approximately:
21 oz. (1,380 yd.) white-with-
blue-flecks, MC
30 oz. (1,970 yd.) navy, CC
Sizes H and J crochet hooks
or sizes to obtain gauge

Finished Size
Approximately 53" x 67"

Gauge
In center, 4 rnds = 4"
In edging pat, 12 sts and
16 rows = 4"

Gauge Swatch
With smaller hook, work as for
Center for 4 rnds.

Pattern Stitch
Long double crochet [Ldc]: Yo,
insert hook from front to back in st
indicated, yo and pull up long lp,
(yo and pull through 2 lps) twice.

Note: *To change colors, work
last yo of prev st with new color,
dropping prev color to ws of
work. Do not fasten off when
changing colors.*

Center
With smaller hook and MC, ch 3;
join with sl st to form ring.
Rnd 1 (rs): Ch 4 [counts as first
dc plus 1 ch throughout], (3 dc in
ring, ch 1) 3 times, 2 dc in ring;
join with sl st to 3rd ch of beg ch-4.
Rnd 2: Sl st in first ch-1 sp, ch 4,
3 dc in same ch-1 sp, ch 1,
* (3 dc, ch 1) twice in next

corner ch-1 sp; rep from *
around, 2 dc in beg ch-1 sp; join
with sl st to 3rd ch of beg ch-4.
Rnd 3: Sl st in first ch-1 sp, ch 4,
3 dc in same ch-1 sp, ch 1,
* 3 dc in next ch-1 sp, ch 1 **,
(3 dc, ch 1) twice in corner
ch-1 sp; rep from * around,
ending last rep at **, 2 dc in beg
ch-1 sp; join with sl st to 3rd ch
of beg ch-4.
Rnds 4–30: Sl st in first ch-1 sp,
ch 4, 3 dc in same ch-1 sp, ch 1,
* (3 dc in next ch-1 sp, ch 1)
across to next corner ch-1 sp **,
(3 dc, ch 1) twice in corner
ch-1 sp; rep from * around,
ending last rep at **, 2 dc in beg
ch-1 sp; join with sl st to 3rd ch
of beg ch-4.
Rnd 31: Sl st in first ch-1 sp,
ch 4, 3 dc in same ch-1 sp, ch 1,

* (3 dc in next ch-1 sp, ch 1) across to next corner ch-1 sp **, (3 dc, ch 1) twice in corner ch-1 sp; rep from * around, ending last rep at **, 2 dc in beg ch-1 sp; change to CC in last st; join with sl st to 3rd ch of beg ch-4; fasten off MC.

Rnds 32–53: With CC, rep rnd 4, 22 times; do not fasten off.

Note: Change to larger hook.

Top Edging

Row 1 (ws): With larger hook and CC, ch 1, turn; sc in same st and in ea dc across, change to MC in last st: 159 sc.

Row 2 (rs): With MC ch 1, turn; sc in first sc and in ea sc across.

Row 3: Ch 1, turn; sc in first sc and in ea st across, change to CC in last st.

Row 4: With CC, ch 1, turn; sc in first 2 sc, Ldc in 3rd sc from beg 3 rows below, * sk next sc on working row, sc in next sc, Ldc in 2nd sc from prev Ldc 3 rows below, sk next sc on working row **, sc in next 5 sc, Ldc in 6th sc from prev Ldc 3 rows below; rep from * across, ending last rep at **, sc in last 2 sc: 40 Ldc.

Row 5: Ch 1, turn; sc in first sc and in ea st across, change to MC in last st.

Row 6: With MC, ch 1, turn; sc in first sc, Ldc in 2nd sc from beg 3 rows below, * sk next sc on working row **, sc in next 3 sc, Ldc in 4th sc from prev Ldc 3 rows below; rep from * across, ending last rep at **, sc in last sc: 40 Ldc.

Row 7: Rep row 3.

Row 8: With CC, ch 1, turn; sc in first 6 sc, Ldc in 7th sc from beg 3 rows below, * sk next sc on working row, sc in next sc, Ldc in 2nd sc from prev Ldc 3 rows below, sk next sc on working row, sc in next 5 sc **, Ldc in 6th sc from prev Ldc 3 rows below; rep from * across, ending last rep at **, sc in last sc: 38 Ldc.

Row 9: Rep row 5.

Row 10: Rep row 6.

Rows 11–28: Rep rows 3–10 twice, then rep rows 3 and 4 once; fasten off after last row.

Bottom Edging

Row 1 (ws): With ws facing and larger hook, join CC in first dc on bottom edge with sl st, ch 1, sc in same st and in ea dc across: 159 sc.

Rows 2–28: Rep rows 2–28 of Top Edging; fasten off MC once; do not fasten off CC.

Border

Rnd 1 (ws): With larger hook and CC, ch 1, turn; 3 sc in last st, sc in ea st across to next corner, 3 sc in corner, sc evenly across to next corner, 3 sc in corner, sc in ea st across to next corner, 3 sc in corner, sc evenly across to next corner; join with sl st st to beg sc.

Rnd 2 (rs): Ch 1, turn; * sc in ea sc across to next corner, 3 sc in corner; rep from * around; join with sl st to beg sc.

Rnd 3 (rs): Sl st in same sc and in ea sc around; join with sl st to beg sl st; fasten off.

Project was stitched by Marge Wild with Wool-ease: Wedgewood Sprinkles #160 and Navy #111.

Rich Ripples

Transform a classic afghan pattern into an upscale throw with luxurious mohair-blend yarn. Mohair is lightweight but very warm.

Finished Size
Approximately 56" x 64"

Gauge
In pat, 11 sts and 12 rows = 4"

Gauge Swatch *(Multiple of 18 sts + 4)*
With MC, ch 40. Work in pat for 16 rows.

Pattern Stitches
Single crochet decrease [sc-dec]: [Worked over 3 sts] Insert hook in st indicated, yo and pull up lp, sk next st, insert hook in next st, yo and pull up lp, yo and pull through all 3 lps on hook.

Long double crochet [Ldc]: Yo, insert hook from front to back in st indicated, yo and pull up long lp, (yo and pull through 2 lps) twice.

Long double crochet decrease [Ldc-dec]: [Worked over 3 sts] Yo, insert hook from front to back in st indicated, yo and pull up long lp, yo and pull through 2 lps, sk next st on working row, insert hook in next st on working row, yo and pull up lp, yo, insert hook from front to back in 4th st from first indicated, yo and pull up long lp,

yo and pull through 2 lps, yo and pull through all 4 lps on hook.

Note: *To change colors, work last yo of prev st with new color, dropping prev color to ws of work. Do not fasten off when changing colors.*

Color sequence: *1 row MC, (2 rows A, 2 rows MC) twice,* * 2 rows B, 2 rows MC, 2 rows A, 2 rows MC, 2 rows B, fasten off B **, (2 rows MC, 2 rows A) 3 times, 2 rows MC, 2 rows B, fasten off B, (2 rows MC, 2 rows A) 3 times, 2 rows MC; rep from * 3 times, then rep from * to ** once, (2 rows MC, 2 rows A) twice, 1 row MC.*

(Continued on page 24)

With MC, ch 148 loosely.

Row 1 (ws): Sc in 2nd ch from hook and in ea ch across: 147 sc.

Row 2 (rs): Ch 1, turn; sc in first sc, 2 sc in next sc, * sc in next 7 sc, sc-dec in next 3 sc, sc in next 7 sc **, 3 sc in next sc; rep from * across to last 2 sc, ending last rep at **, 2 sc in next sc, sc in last sc: 147 sts.

Row 3 and all Odd Rows: Ch 1, turn; sc in first sc and in ea st across.

Row 4: Ch 1, turn; sc in first 2 sc, Ldc in first sc 3 rows below, sc in next sc on working row, Ldc in 2nd sc from prev Ldc 3 rows below, sk next sc on working row, sc in next sc, * (Ldc in 2nd sc from prev Ldc 3 rows below, sk next sc on working row, sc in next sc) twice, Ldc-dec beg in 2nd sc from prev Ldc 3 rows below, (sk next sc on working row, sc in next sc, Ldc in 2nd sc from prev Ldc 3 rows below) 3 times, sk next sc on working row, sc in next sc, Ldc in next sc from prev Ldc 3 rows below **, sc in next sc on working row, Ldc in same sc as prev Ldc 3 rows below, sc in next sc, Ldc in next sc from prev Ldc 3 rows below, sk next sc on working row, sc in next sc; rep from * across, ending last rep at **, sc in last 2 sc: 147 sts.

Rows 5–188: Rep rows 3 and 4, 92 times; do not turn after last row; fasten of A and B; do not fasten off MC.

Border

Rnd 1 (rs): With rs facing and MC, ch 1, 3 sc in last st, sc evenly across to next corner, 3 sc in corner, (sc in ea ch across to next peak, 3 sc in peak, sc in ea ch across to next valley, sc-dec in next 3 ch) across to next corner, 3 sc in corner, sc evenly across to next corner, 3 sc in corner, (sc in ea st across to next valley, sc-dec in next 3 sts, sc in ea st across to next peak, 3 sc in peak) across to next corner; join with sl st to beg sc; fasten off.

Rnd 2 (ws): With ws facing, join B in any corner with sl st, ch 1, * sc in ea sc across to next corner, 3 sc in corner; rep from * around; join with sl st to beg sc; fasten off.

Rnd 3 (rs): With rs facing, join MC in top left corner with sl st, ch 1, 3 sc in same st, sc in ea sc across to next corner, 3 sc in corner, (sc in ea sc across to next peak, 3 sc in peak, sc in ea sc across to next valley, sc-dec in next 3 sc) across to next corner, 3 sc in corner, sc in ea sc across to next corner, 3 sc in corner, (sc in ea sc across to next valley, sc-dec in next 3 sts, sc in ea sc across to next peak, 3 sc in peak) across to next corner; join with sl st to beg sc; fasten off.

Rnd 4 (ws): With A, rep rnd 2.

Rnd 5 (rs): Rep rnd 3.

Project was stitched by Joann Moss with Imagine: Blue on Blue #340, Mulberry #190, and Maize #186.

Golden Bouquets

Rows of yellow blooms show up nicely in oversize navy blocks. Edge each block with double crochet stitches before joining them together.

Materials

Worsted-weight wool-blend yarn, approximately:
30 oz. (1,970 yd.) navy, MC
27 oz. (1,775 yd.) gold, CC
Size J crochet hook or size to obtain gauge
Yarn needle

Finished Size

Approximately 59" x 72"

Gauge

In pat, 11 sts and 15 rows = 4"
Ea Block = 18" x 19½"

Gauge Swatch (Multiple of 8 sts)

With CC, ch 24. Work in pat for 20 rows.

Pattern Stitch

Long double crochet [Ldc]: Yo, insert hook from front to back in st indicated, yo and pull up long lp, (yo and pull through 2 lps) twice.

Note: To change colors, work last yo of prev st with new color, dropping prev color to ws of work. Do not fasten off when changing colors.

Block (Make 12.)

With CC, ch 48 loosely.

Row 1 (ws): Sc in 2nd ch from hook and in ea ch across, change to MC in last st: 47 sc.

Row 2 (rs): With MC, ch 1, turn; sc in first sc and in ea sc across.

Row 3: Ch 1, turn; sc in first sc and in ea st across, change to CC in last st.

Row 4: With CC, ch 1, turn; sc in first sc, Ldc in 4th sc from beg 3 rows below, * (sk next sc on working row, sc in next sc, Ldc in same sc as prev Ldc 3 rows below) twice **, (sk next sc on working row, sc in next sc, Ldc in 4th sc from prev Ldc 3 rows below) twice; rep from * across, ending last rep at **, sk next sc on working row, sc in last sc: 23 Ldc.

Row 5: Ch 1, turn; sc in first sc and in ea st across, change to MC in last st.

Row 6: With MC, ch 1, turn; sc in first 2 sc, Ldc in 3rd sc from beg 3 rows below, * sk next sc on working row, sc in next sc **, Ldc in 2nd sc from prev Ldc 3 rows below; rep from * across, ending last rep at **, sc in last sc: 22 Ldc.

Rows 7–56: Rep rows 3–6, 12 times, then rep rows 3 and 4 once; do not turn after last row; fasten off CC; do not fasten off MC.

Edging

Rnd 1 (rs): With rs facing and MC, sl st in first sc, ch 1, 3 sc in last st, sc in ea st across to corner [45 sc], 3 sc in corner, work 36 sc evenly across to next corner, 3 sc in corner, sc in ea ch across to next corner [45 sc], 3 sc in corner, work 36 sc evenly across to next corner; join with sl st to beg sc: 174 sc.

Rnd 2 (ws): Ch 1, turn; * sc in ea sc across to next corner, 3 sc in corner; rep from * around; join with sl st to beg sc; fasten off: 182 sc.

Rnd 3 (rs): With rs facing, join CC in any corner with sl st, ch 3 [counts as first dc], dc in same sc and in ea sc across to next corner, * 3 dc in corner, dc in ea sc across to next corner; rep from * around, dc in same sc as beg ch-3; join with sl st to to 3rd ch of beg ch-3; fasten off: 190 dc.

Rnd 4 (ws): With ws facing, join MC in any corner with sl st, ch 1, * 3 sc in corner, sc in ea dc across to next corner; rep from * around; join with sl st to beg sc: 198 sc.

Rnd 5 (rs): Ch 1, turn; * sc in ea sc across to next corner, 3 sc in corner; rep from * around; join with sl st to beg sc; fasten off: 206 sc.

Assembly

Afghan is 4 blocks long and 3 blocks wide. With ws facing and using MC, whipstitch blocks tog.

Border

With ws facing, join MC in any corner with sl st, ch 1, * sc in ea st across to next corner, 3 sc in corner; rep from * around; join with sl st to beg sc; fasten off.

Project was stitched by Margarete Dahlke with Wool-ease: Navy #111 and Butterscotch #189.

Stylish Stole and Hat

Stitch a lovely wrap for a chilly day or, if you prefer, use the alternative instructions to make a smaller scarf. Then complete the look with a simple hat that sports a matching brim.

Stole

Materials
Worsted-weight mohair-blend yarn, approximately:
Stole: 10 oz. (890 yd.) black, MC
12 oz. (1,075 yd.) purple, CC
Scarf: 5 oz. (445 yd.) black, MC
6 oz. (540 yd.) purple, CC
Size J crochet hook or size to obtain gauge

Finished Size
Stole: Approximately 22" x 69"
Scarf: Approximately 10" x 69"

Gauge
In pat, 8 sts and 11 rows = 3"

Gauge Swatch *(Multiple of 8 sts + 4)*
With MC, ch 20. Work in pat for 14 rows.

Pattern Stitch
Long double crochet [Ldc]: Yo, insert hook from front to back in st indicated, yo and pull up long lp, (yo and pull through 2 lps) twice.

Note: Directions are written for Stole, with Scarf in braces. To change colors, work last yo of prev st with new color, dropping prev color to ws of work. Do not fasten off when changing colors.

With MC, ch 60 {28} loosely.
Row 1 (ws): Sc in 2nd ch from hook and in ea ch across, change to CC in last st: 59 {27} sc.
Row 2 (rs): With CC, ch 1, turn; sc in first sc and in ea sc across.
Row 3: Ch 1, turn; sc in first sc and in ea st across, change to MC in last st.
Row 4: With MC, ch 1, turn; sc in first sc, Ldc in 2nd sc from beg 3 rows below, * sk next sc on working row, sc in next sc **, Ldc in 2nd sc from prev Ldc 3 rows below; rep from * across, ending last rep at **: 29 {13} Ldc.
Row 5: Ch 1, turn; sc in first sc and in ea st across, change to CC in last st.
Row 6: With CC, ch 1, turn; sc in first 2 sc, Ldc in 5th sc from beg 3 rows below [slant-st made], * sk next sc on working row, sc in next sc, Ldc in same sc as prev Ldc 3 rows below, sk next sc on working row, sc in next sc, Ldc in 2nd sc from prev Ldc 3 rows below, sk next sc on working row, sc in next sc, Ldc in same sc as prev Ldc 3 rows below [slant-st made], sk next sc on working row, sc in next sc **, Ldc in 6th sc from prev Ldc 3 rows below [slant-st made]; rep from * across, ending last rep at **, sc in last sc: 14 {6} Ldc and 14 {6} slant-sts.
Rows 7–9: Rep rows 3–5 once.
Row 10: With CC, ch 1, turn; sc in first 2 sc, Ldc in 3rd sc from beg 3 rows below, * sk next sc on working row, sc in next sc, Ldc in same sc as prev Ldc 3 rows below [slant-st made], sk next sc on working row, sc in next sc, Ldc in 6th sc from prev Ldc 3 rows below [slant-st made], sk next sc on working row, sc in next sc, Ldc in same sc as prev Ldc 3 rows below, sk next sc on working row, sc in next sc **, Ldc in 2nd sc from prev Ldc 3 rows below; rep from * across, ending last rep at **, sc in last sc: 14 {6} Ldc and 14 {6} slant-sts.
Rows 11–252: Rep rows 3–10, 30 times, then rep rows 3 and 4 once; do not turn after last row; fasten of CC; do not fasten off MC.

Border
Rnd 1 (rs): With rs facing and MC, ch 1, 3 sc in last st, sc evenly across to next corner, 3 sc in corner, sc in ea ch across to next corner, 3 sc in corner, sc evenly across to next corner, 3 sc in corner, sc in ea st across to next corner; join with sl st to beg sc.
Rnd 2 (ws): Ch 1, turn; * sc in ea sc across to corner, 3 sc in corner; rep from * around; join with sl st to beg sc.
Rnd 3 (rs): Turn; sl st in same sc and in ea sc around; join with sl st to beg sl st; fasten off.

Project was stitched by Joann Moss with Imagine: Black #153 and Purple Haze #338.

Hat

Materials
Worsted-weight mohair-blend yarn, approximately:
2½ oz. (225 yd.) black, MC
2 oz. (1,80 yd.) purple, CC
Size J crochet hook or size to obtain gauge

Finished Size
Approximately 24" in diameter

Gauge
8 hdc and 5 rnds = 3"

Gauge Swatch
Work in pat for 6 rnds.

Pattern Stitch
Long double crochet [Ldc]: Yo, insert hook from front to back in st indicated, yo and pull up long lp, (yo and pull through 2 lps) twice.

Note: To change colors, work last yo of prev st with new color, dropping prev color to ws of work. Do not fasten off when changing colors.

With MC, ch 3.
Note: Do not join rnds. Place marker at beg of ea rnd. Mark first rnd as rs.

Rnd 1 (rs): Work 8 hdc in 3rd ch from hook: 8 hdc.
Rnd 2: Work 2 hdc in first hdc and in ea hdc around: 16 hdc.
Rnd 3: Hdc in first hdc, * 2 hdc in next hdc, hdc in next hdc; rep from * around, 2 hdc in last hdc: 24 hdc.
Rnd 4: Hdc in first 2 hdc, * 2 hdc in next hdc, hdc in next 2 hdc; rep from * around, 2 hdc in last hdc: 32 hdc.
Rnd 5: Hdc in first 3 hdc, * 2 hdc in next hdc, hdc in next 3 hdc; rep from * around, 2 hdc in last hdc: 40 hdc.
Rnd 6: Hdc in first 4 hdc, * 2 hdc in next hdc, hdc in next 4 hdc; rep from * around, 2 hdc in last hdc: 48 hdc.
Rnd 7: Hdc in first hdc and in ea hdc around: 48 hdc.
Rnd 8: Hdc in first 5 hdc, * 2 hdc in next hdc, hdc in next 5 hdc; rep from * around, 2 hdc in last hdc: 56 hdc.
Rnd 9: Rep rnd 7: 56 hdc.
Rnd 10: Hdc in first 6 hdc, * 2 hdc in next hdc, hdc in next 6 hdc; rep from * around, 2 hdc in last hdc: 64 hdc.
Rnds 11–16: Rep rnd 7, 6 times: 64 hdc.

Note: Beg joining rnds.

Rnd 17 (rs): Sc in first hdc and in ea hdc around, change to CC in last st; join with sl st to beg sc: 64 sc.
Rnd 18 (ws): With CC, ch 1, turn; sc in first sc and in ea sc around; join with sl st to beg sc.
Rnd 19: Ch 1, turn; sc in first sc and in ea sc around; join with sl st to beg sc, change to MC in last st.
Rnd 20: With MC, ch 1, turn; sc in first sc, Ldc in 2nd sc from beg 3 rows below, * sk next sc on working row, sc in next sc, Ldc in 2nd sc from prev Ldc 3 rows below; rep from * around; join with sl st to beg sc: 32 Ldc.
Rnd 21: Ch 1, turn; sc in first sc and in ea st around; join with sl st to beg sc, change to CC in last st.
Rnd 22: With CC, ch 1, turn; Ldc in 3rd sc from beg 3 rows below [slant-st made], * sk next sc on working row, sc in next sc, Ldc in same sc as prev Ldc 3 rows below, sk next sc on working row, sc in next sc, Ldc in 2nd sc from prev Ldc 3 rows below, sk next sc on working row, sc in next sc, Ldc in same sc as prev Ldc 3 rows below [slant-st made], sk next sc on working row, sc in next sc **, Ldc in 6th sc from prev Ldc 3 rows below [slant-st made]; rep from * around, ending last rep at **; join with sl st to beg Ldc: 16 Ldc and 16 slant-sts.
Rnds 23–25: Rep rnds 19–21 once.
Rnd 26: With CC, ch 1, turn; Ldc in first sc 3 rows below, * sk next sc on working row, sc in next sc, Ldc in same sc as prev Ldc 3 rows below [slant-st made], sk next sc on working row, sc in next sc, Ldc in 6th sc from prev Ldc 3 rows below [slant-st made], sk next sc on working row, sc in next sc, Ldc in same sc as prev Ldc 3 rows below, sk next sc on working row, sc in next sc **, Ldc in 2nd sc from prev Ldc 3 rows below; rep from * around, ending last rep at **; join with sl st to beg Ldc: 16 Ldc and 16 slant-sts.
Rnds 27–32: Rep rnds 19–23 once, then rep rnd 20 once.
Rnd 33: Turn; sl st in first st and in ea st around; join with sl st to beg sl st; fasten off.
Fold up contrasting brim.

Project was stitched by Lily M. Chin with Imagine: Black #153 and Purple Haze #338.

Bright and Bold

Electric blue and shocking pink yarns give these zigzags extra zip.
Finish each point with a giant tassel.

Materials

Sportweight acrylic microfiber yarn, approximately:
27½ oz. (1,850 yd.) blue, MC
25 oz. (1,680 yd.) pink, CC
Size I crochet hook or size to obtain gauge

Finished Size

Approximately 46" x 51"

Gauge

In pat, 14 sts and 15 rows = 4½"

Gauge Swatch *(Multiple of 14 sts + 4)*

With MC, ch 32. Work in pat for 20 rows.

Pattern Stitches

Single crochet decrease [sc-dec]: [Worked over 3 sts] Insert hook in st indicated, yo and pull up lp, sk next st, insert hook in next st, yo and pull up lp, yo and pull through all 3 lps on hook.

Long double crochet [Ldc]: Yo, insert hook from front to back in st indicated, yo and pull up long lp, (yo and pull through 2 lps) twice.

Long double crochet decrease [Ldc-dec]: [Worked over 3 sts] Yo, insert hook from front to back in st indicated, yo and pull up long lp, yo and pull through 2 lps, sk next st on working row, insert hook in next st on working row, yo and pull up lp, yo, insert hook from front to back in 4th st from first st indicated, yo and pull up long lp, yo and pull through 2 lps, yo and pull through all 4 lps on hook.

Note: *To change colors, work last yo of prev st with new color, dropping prev color to ws of work. Do not fasten off when changing colors.*

With MC, ch 144 loosely.

Row 1 (ws): Sc in 2nd ch from hook and in ea ch across, change to CC in last st: 143 sc.

Row 2 (rs): With CC, ch 1, turn; sc in first sc, 2 sc in next sc, * sc in next 5 sc, sc-dec in next 3 sc, sc in next 5 sc **, 3 sc in next sc; rep from * across, ending last rep at **, 2 sc in next sc, sc in last sc: 143 sts.

Row 3: Ch 1, turn; sc in first sc and in ea st across, change to MC in last st.

Row 4: With MC, ch 1, turn; sc in first 2 sc, Ldc in 2nd sc from beg 3 rows below, * sc in next sc on working row, Ldc in next sc from prev Ldc 3 rows below, sk next sc on working row, sc in next sc, Ldc in 2nd sc from prev Ldc 3 rows below, sk next sc on working row, sc in next sc, Ldc-dec beg in 2nd sc from prev Ldc 3 rows below, (sk next sc on working row, sc in next sc, Ldc in 2nd sc from prev Ldc 3 rows below) twice, sk next sc on working row, sc in next sc, Ldc in next sc from prev Ldc 3 rows below **, sk next sc on working row, sc in next sc, Ldc in same sc as prev Ldc 3 rows below; rep from * across, ending last rep at **, sc in last 2 sc: 143 sts.

Row 5: Ch 1, turn; sc in first sc and in ea st across, change to CC in last st.

Row 6: With CC, rep row 4.

Rows 7–168: Rep rows 3–6, 40 times, then rep rows 3 and 4 once; do not turn after last row; fasten of CC; do not fasten off MC.

Border

Rnd 1 (rs): With rs facing and MC, ch 1, 3 sc in last st, sc evenly across to next corner, 3 sc in corner, (sc in ea ch across to next peak, 3 sc in peak, sc in ea ch across to next valley, sc-dec in next 3 ch) across to next corner, 3 sc in corner, sc evenly across to next corner, 3 sc in corner, (sc in ea st across to next valley, sc-dec in next 3 sts, sc in ea st across to next peak, 3 sc in peak) across to next corner; join with sl st to beg sc.

Rnd 2 (rs): With rs facing, sl st in same st and in ea st around; join with sl st to beg sc; fasten off.

Tassels

For ea tassel, referring to page 143 of General Directions, wind yarn around 8" piece of cardboard 60 times. Working across short ends, join 1 tassel to ea point, alternating colors.

Project was stitched Joann Moss with Microspun: Turquoise #148 and Fuchsia #146.

Rainbow Stripes

Capture the beauty of a rainbow with muted colors and simple X-stitches.
Tie it all up with a multicolored border.

Materials
Worsted-weight wool-blend
yarn, approximately:
18 oz. (1,185 yd.) cream, MC
6 oz. (395 yd.) purple, A
6 oz. (395 yd.) blue, B
6 oz. (395 yd.) green, C
6 oz. (395 yd.) yellow, D
6 oz. (395 yd.) red, E
6 oz. (395 yd.) pink, F
Size J crochet hook or size to
obtain gauge

Finished Size
Approximately 51" x 60½"

Gauge
In pat, 11½ sts and 15 rows = 4"

Gauge Swatch *(Multiple of 4 sts + 2)*
With A, ch 18. Work in pat for 20
rows.

Pattern Stitch
Long double crochet [Ldc]: Yo,
insert hook from front to back in
st indicated, yo and pull up long
lp, (yo and pull through 2 lps)
twice.

Note: *To change colors, work
last yo of prev st with new color,
dropping prev color to ws of
work. Do not fasten off when
changing colors.*

Color sequence: *1 row A,
(2 rows MC, 2 rows A) 3 times,
2 rows MC, 1 row A, 1 row B,
(2 rows MC, 2 rows B) 3 times,
2 rows MC, 1 row B, 1 row C,
(2 rows MC, 2 rows C) 3 times,
2 rows MC, 1 row C, 1 row D,
(2 rows MC, 2 rows D) 3 times,
2 rows MC, 1 row D, 1 row E,
(2 rows MC, 2 rows E) 3 times,
2 rows MC, 1 row E, 1 row F,
(2 rows MC, 2 rows F) 3 times,
2 rows MC, 1 row F, 1 row A,
(2 rows MC, 2 rows A) 3 times,
2 rows MC, 1 row A, 1 row F,
(2 rows MC, 2 rows F) 3 times,
2 rows MC, 1 row F, 1 row E,
(2 rows MC, 2 rows E) 3 times,
2 rows MC, 1 row E, 1 row D,
(2 rows MC, 2 rows D) 3 times,
2 rows MC, 1 row D, 1 row C,
(2 rows MC, 2 rows C) 3 times,
2 rows MC, 1 row C, 1 row B,
(2 rows MC, 2 rows B) 3 times,
2 rows MC, 1 row B, 1 row A,
(2 rows MC, 2 rows A) 3 times,
2 rows MC, 1 row A.*

With A, ch 134 loosely.
Row 1 (ws): Sc in 2nd ch from
hook and in ea ch across: 133 sc.
Row 2 (rs): Ch 1, turn; sc in first
sc and in ea sc across.
Row 3 and all Odd Rows: Ch 1,
turn; sc in first sc and in ea st
across.
Row 4: Ch 1, turn; sc in first sc,
Ldc in 4th sc from beg 3 rows

below, * sk next sc on working
row, sc in next sc, Ldc in 2nd sc
before prev Ldc 3 rows below
[X-st made], sk next sc on working row, sc in next sc **, Ldc in
4th sc from prev Ldc 3 rows
below; rep from * across, ending
last rep at **: 33 X-sts.
Row 6: Ch 1, turn; sc in first 2 sc,
Ldc in 3rd sc from beg 3 rows
below, * sk next sc on working
row, sc in next sc **, Ldc in 2nd
sc from prev Ldc 3 rows below;
rep from * across, ending last rep
at **, sc in last sc: 65 Ldc.
Rows 7–208: Rep rows 3–6, 50
times, then rep rows 3 and 4
once; fasten off.

Border
Rnd 1 (rs): With rs facing, join
MC, in top right corner with sl st,
ch 1, 3 sc in corner, sc in ea sc
across to next corner, 3 sc in
corner, sc evenly across to next
corner, 3 sc in corner, sc in ea ch
across to next corner, 3 sc in
corner, sc evenly across to next
corner; join with sl st to beg sc;
fasten off.
Rnd 2 (ws): With ws facing, join
F in any corner with sl st, ch 1,
* 3 sc in corner, sc in ea sc across
to next corner; rep from *
around; join with sl st to beg sc;
fasten off.

(Continued on page 36)

Rnd 3 and all Odd Rnds (rs): With rs facing, join MC in any corner with sl st, ch 1, * 3 sc in corner, sc in ea sc across to next corner; rep from * around; join with sl st to beg sc; fasten off.

Rnd 4 (ws): With E, rep rnd 2.

Rnd 6 (ws): With D, rep rnd 2.

Rnd 8 (ws): With C, rep rnd 2.

Rnd 10 (ws): With B, rep rnd 2.

Rnd 12 (ws): With A, rep rnd 2; do not fasten off.

Rnd 13 (rs): With A, turn; sl st in first sc and in ea sc around; join with sl st to beg sl st; fasten off.

Project was stitched by Marge Scensny with Wool-ease: Natural Heather #98, Grape Heather #144, Blue Heather #107, Green Heather #130, Butterscotch #189, Tapestry Heather #141, and Rose Heather #140.

Pink Pistachio

This afghan is a sweet confection of ice-cream colors and lots of fringe.

Materials

Chunky-weight brushed acrylic yarn, approximately:
27 oz. (1,215 yd.) pink, MC
18 oz. (810 yd.) mint, CC
Size K crochet hook or size to obtain gauge

Finished Size

Approximately 46" x 50", without fringe

Gauge

In pat, 12 sts and 15 rows = 5"

Gauge Swatch *(Multiple of 6 sts + 2)*

With CC, ch 20. Work in pat for 24 rows.

Pattern Stitch

Long double crochet [Ldc]: Yo, insert hook from front to back in st indicated, yo and pull up long lp, (yo and pull through 2 lps) twice.

Note: To change colors, work last yo of prev st with new color, dropping prev color to ws of work. Do not fasten off when changing colors.

*Color sequence: 1 row CC, (2 rows MC, 2 rows CC) 7 times, fasten off CC, * 14 rows MC, 2 rows CC, (2 rows MC, 2 rows CC) 6 times fasten off CC; rep from * once, 14 rows MC, 2 rows CC, (2 rows MC, 2 rows CC) 5 times, 2 rows MC, 1 row CC.*

With CC, ch 110 loosely.
Row 1 (ws): Sc in 2nd ch from hook and in ea ch across: 109 sc.
Row 2 (rs): Ch 1, turn; sc in first sc and in ea sc across.
Row 3 and all Odd Rows: Ch 1, turn; sc in first sc and in ea st across.

Row 4: Ch 1, turn; sc in first sc, Ldc in 2nd sc from beg 3 rows below, * sk next sc on working row, sc in next 5 sc **, Ldc in 6th sc from prev Ldc 3 rows below; rep from * across, ending last rep at **: 18 Ldc.

Row 6: Ch 1, turn; sc in first 2 sc, Ldc in 3rd sc from beg 3 rows below, * sk next sc on working row **, sc in next 5 sc, Ldc in 6th sc from prev Ldc 3 rows below; rep from * across, ending last rep at **, sc in last 4 sc: 18 Ldc.

Row 8: Ch 1, turn; sc in first 3 sc, Ldc in 4th sc from beg 3 rows below, * sk next sc on working row **, sc in next 5 sc, Ldc in 6th sc from prev Ldc 3 rows below; rep from * across, ending last rep at **, sc in last 3 sc: 18 Ldc.

Row 10: Ch 1, turn; sc in first 4 sc, Ldc in 5th sc from beg 3 rows below, * sk next sc on working row **, sc in next 5 sc, Ldc in 6th sc from prev Ldc 3 rows below; rep from * across, ending last rep at **, sc in last 2 sc: 18 Ldc.

Row 12: Ch 1, turn; sc in first 5 sc, Ldc in 6th sc from beg 3 rows below, * sk next sc on working row **, sc in next 5 sc, Ldc in 6th sc from prev Ldc 3 rows below; rep from * across, ending last rep at **, sc in last sc: 18 Ldc.

Row 14: Ch 1, turn; sc in first 6 sc, Ldc in 7th sc from beg 3 rows below, * sk next sc on working row, sc in next 5 sc **, Ldc in 6th sc from prev Ldc 3 rows below; rep from * across, ending last rep at **, sc in last sc: 17 Ldc.

Rows 15–42: Rep rows 3–14 twice, then rep rows 3–6 once.

Row 44: Rep row 4.
Row 46: Rep row 14.
Row 48: Rep row 12.
Row 50: Rep row 10.
Row 52: Rep row 8.
Row 54: Rep row 6.
Rows 55–78: Rep rows 43–54 twice.
Row 80: Rep row 4.
Row 82: Rep row 14.
Rows 83–148: Rep rows 3–68 once; do not turn after last row; fasten off MC; do not fasten off CC.

Border

With rs facing and CC, ch 1, 3 sc in last st, sc evenly across to next corner, 3 sc in corner, sc in ea ch across to next corner, 3 sc in corner, sc evenly across to next corner, 3 sc in corner, sc in ea st across to next corner; join with sl st to beg sc; fasten off.

Fringe

For ea tassel, referring to page 143 of General Directions, cut 2 (12") lengths of MC. Working across short ends, knot 1 tassel in ea st.

Project was stitched by Madeline Speziale with Jiffy: Baby Pink #104 and Pistachio #169.

Americana

Show your patriotism with these rippling stripes of red, white, and blue.

Materials

Worsted-weight wool-blend yarn, approximately:
27 oz. (1,775 yd.) red, MC
18 oz. (1,185 yd.) blue, A
6 oz. (395 yd.) white, B
Size J crochet hook or size to obtain gauge

Finished Size

Approximately 53" x 64"

Gauge

In pat, 11 sts and 14 rows = 4"

Gauge Swatch *(Multiple of 4 sts + 2)*

With MC, ch 22. Work in pat for 19 rows.

Pattern Stitch

Long double crochet [Ldc]: Yo, insert hook from front to back in st indicated, yo and pull up long lp, (yo and pull through 2 lps) twice.

Note: *To change colors, work last yo of prev st with new color, dropping prev color to ws of work. Do not fasten off when changing colors.*

Color sequence: *1 row MC, (2 rows A, 2 rows MC) 3 times, * 2 rows B, fasten off B, (2 rows MC, 2 rows A) 3 times **, 2 rows MC; rep from * 12 times, ending last rep at **, 1 row MC.*

With MC, ch 142 loosely.
Row 1 (ws): Sc in 2nd ch from hook and in ea ch across: 141 sc.
Row 2 (rs): Ch 1, turn; sc in first sc and in ea sc across.

Row 3 and all Odd Rows: Ch 1, turn; sc in first sc and in ea st across.
Row 4: Ch 1, turn; sc in first sc, Ldc in 4th sc from beg 3 rows below, * sk next sc on working row, sc in next sc, Ldc in 2nd sc before prev Ldc 3 rows below [X-st made], sk next sc on working row, sc in next sc **, Ldc in 3rd sc from prev Ldc 3 rows below, sk next sc on working row, sc in next sc, Ldc in same sc as prev Ldc 3 rows below [V-st made], sk next sc on working row, sc in next sc, Ldc in 5th sc from prev Ldc 3 rows below; rep from * across, ending last rep at **: 18 X-sts and 17 V-sts.
Row 6: Ch 1, turn; sc in first 2 sc, Ldc in 3rd sc from beg 3 rows below, * sk next sc on working row, sc in next 2 sc **, Ldc in 4th sc from prev Ldc 3 rows below, sk next sc on working row, sc in next sc, Ldc in same sc as prev Ldc 3 rows below [V-st made], sk next sc on working row, sc in next 2 sc, Ldc in 4th sc from prev Ldc 3 rows below; rep from * across, ending last rep at **: 18 Ldc and 17 V-sts.

Rows 7–220: Rep rows 3–6, 53 times, then rep rows 3 and 4 once; fasten off after last row.

Border

Rnd 1 (ws): With ws facing, join A in any corner with sl st, ch 1, * 3 sc in corner, sc evenly across to next corner; rep from * around; join with sl st to beg sc; fasten off.
Rnd 2 (rs): With rs facing, join B in any corner with sl st, ch 1, * 3 sc in corner, sc in ea sc across to next corner; rep from * around; join with sl st to beg sc; fasten off.
Rnd 3 (ws): With ws facing, join MC in any corner with sl st, ch 1, sc in same st and in ea sc across to next corner, * 3 sc in corner, sc in ea sc across to next corner; rep from * around, 2 sc in corner; join with sl st to beg sc.
Rnd 4 (rs): Ch 1, turn; working from left to right, sc in same st and in ea sc around; join with sl st to beg sc; fasten off.

Project was stitched by Margarete Dahlke with Wool-ease: Ranch Red #102, Navy #111, and White #100.

Tea Cozy and Place Mat

It's time for tea with this charming cozy. Make a matching place mat for everyone in your tea party.

Tea Cozy

Materials

Worsted-weight cotton yarn, approximately:
5 oz. (240 yd.) blue, MC
5 oz. (240 yd.) yellow, CC
Size H crochet hook or size to obtain gauge

Finished Size

Approximately 24" in circumference and 12" high

Gauge

In pat, 12 sts and 16 rows = 4"

Gauge Swatch *(Multiple of 10 sts + 8)*

With MC, ch 18. Work in pat for 20 rows.

Pattern Stitches

Long double crochet [Ldc]: Yo, insert hook from front to back in st indicated, yo and pull up long lp, (yo and pull through 2 lps) twice.

Front Post Double Crochet [FPdc]: Yo, insert hook from front to back around post of st indicated, yo and pull up lp, (yo and pull through 2 lps) twice.

Decrease [dec]: [Worked over 2 sts] Insert hook in st indicated and pull up lp, insert hook in next st and pull up lp, yo and pull through all 3 lps on hook.

Note: To change colors, work last yo of prev st with new color, dropping prev color to ws of work. Do not fasten off when changing colors.

Tea Cozy Front

With MC, ch 38 loosely.

Row 1 (ws): Sc in 2nd ch from hook and in ea ch across, change to CC in last st: 37 sc.

Row 2 (rs): With CC, ch 1, turn; sc in first sc and in ea sc across.

Row 3: Ch 1, turn; sc in first sc and in ea st across, change to MC in last st.

Row 4: With MC, ch 1, turn; sc in first 2 sc, Ldc in 4th sc from beg 3 rows below, * sk next sc on working row, sc in next sc, Ldc in same sc as prev Ldc [V-st made], sk next sc on working row **, sc in next 3 sc, Ldc in 5th sc from prev Ldc 3 rows below, sk next sc on working row, sc in next 3 sc, Ldc in 5th sc from prev Ldc 3 rows below; rep from * across, ending last rep at **, sc in last 2 sc: 4 V-sts and 3 Ldc.

Row 5: Ch 1, turn; sc in first sc and in ea st across, change to CC in last st.

Row 6: With CC, ch 1, turn; sc in first 3 sc, Ldc in 4th sc from beg 3 rows below, * sk next sc on working row, sc in next 3 sc **, FPdc around next Ldc 3 rows below, sk next sc on working row, sc in next sc, FPdc around same Ldc as last FPdc [V-st made], sk next sc on working row, sc in next 3 sc, Ldc in 5th sc from prev FPdc 3 rows below; rep from * across, ending last rep at **: 3 V-sts and 4 Ldc.

Row 7: Rep row 3.

Row 8: With MC, ch 1, turn; sc in first 2 sc, * FPdc around next Ldc 3 rows below, sk next sc on working row, sc in next sc, FPdc around same Ldc as prev FPdc [V-st made], sk next sc on working row **, sc in next 3 sc, Ldc in 5th sc from prev FPdc 3 rows below, sk next sc on working row, sc in next 3 sc; rep from * across, ending last rep at **, sc in last 2 sc: 4 V-sts and 3 Ldc.

Rows 9–36: Rep rows 5–8, 7 times.

Row 37: With MC, ch 1, turn; sc in first 5 sts, dec in next 2 sts, (sc in next 3 sts, dec in next 2 sts) across to last 5 sts, sc in last 5 sts, change to CC in last st: 31 sts.

Row 38: With CC, ch 1, turn; sc in first 3 sc, Ldc in 4th sc from beg 3 rows below, * sk next sc on working row, sc in next 2 sc **, FPdc around next Ldc 3 rows below, sk next sc on working row, sc in next sc, FPdc around same Ldc as last FPdc [V-st made], sk next sc on working row, sc in next 2 sc, Ldc in 4th sc from prev FPdc 3 rows below; rep from * across, ending last rep at **, sc in last sc: 3 V-sts and 4 Ldc.

Row 39: Rep row 3.

Row 40: With MC, ch 1, turn; sc in first 2 sc, * FPdc around next Ldc 3 rows below, sk next sc on working row, sc in next sc, FPdc around same Ldc as prev FPdc [V-st made], sk next sc on working row, sc in next 2 sc **, Ldc in 4th sc from prev FPdc 3 rows below, sk next sc on working row, sc in next 2 sc; rep from * across, ending last rep at **: 4 V-sts and 3 Ldc.

Row 41: Rep row 5.

Row 42: Rep row 38.

Row 43: Ch 1, turn; sc in first sc,

(Continued on page 44)

(dec in next 2 sts, sc in next st) twice, (dec in next 2 sts, sc in next 3 sts) across to last 9 sts, (dec in next 2 sts, sc in next st) 3 times, change to MC in last st: 23 sts.

Row 44: With MC, ch 1, turn; sc in first sc, * FPdc around next Ldc 3 rows below, sk next sc on working row, sc in next sc, FPdc around same Ldc as prev FPdc 3 rows below [V-st made], sk next sc on working row, sc in next sc **, Ldc in 3rd sc from prev FPdc 3 rows below, sk next sc on working row, sc in next sc; rep from * across, ending last rep at **: 4 V-sts and 3 Ldc.

Row 45: Rep row 5.

Row 46: With CC, ch 1, turn; sc in first 2 sc, Ldc in 3rd sc from beg 3 rows below, * sk next sc on working row, sc in next sc **, FPdc around next Ldc 3 rows below, sk next sc on working row, sc in next sc, FPdc around same Ldc as prev FPdc [V-st made], sk next sc on working row, sc in next sc, Ldc in 3rd sc from prev FPdc 3 rows below; rep from * across, ending last rep at **, sc in last sc: 3 V-sts and 4 Ldc.

Row 47: Rep row 3.

Row 48: Rep row 44; fasten off.

Tea Cozy Back
Work as for Tea Cozy Front.

Assembly
With rs facing, whipstitch Front to Back, leaving bottom open and leaving spaces in side seams for teapot spout and handle.

Border
Rnd 1 (ws): With ws facing, join CC in any st along bottom edge with sl st, ch 1, sc in same st and in ea st around; join with sl st to beg sc; fasten off.

Rnd 2 (rs): With rs facing, join MC in any st along bottom edge with sl st, ch 1, sc in same sc and in ea sc around; join with sl st to beg sc; fasten off.

Project was stitched by Lily M. Chin with Kitchen Cotton: Morning Glory Blue #108 and Sunflower #157.

Place Mat

Finished Size
Approximately 18" x 13"

Gauge
In pat, 12 sts and 16 rows = 4"

Gauge Swatch *(Multiple of 8 sts + 6)*
With MC, ch 22. Work in pat for 20 rows.

Pattern Stitches
Long double crochet [Ldc]:
Yo, insert hook from front to back in st indicated, yo and pull up long lp, (yo and pull through 2 lps) twice.

Front Post Double Crochet [FPdc]: Yo, insert hook from front to back around post of st indicated, yo and pull up lp, (yo and pull through 2 lps) twice.

Note: To change colors, work last yo of prev st with new color, dropping prev color to ws of work. Do not fasten off when changing colors.

With MC, ch 54 loosely.
Row 1 (ws): Sc in 2nd ch from hook and in ea ch across, change to CC in last st: 53 sc.

Row 2 (rs): With CC, ch 1, turn; sc in first sc and in ea sc across.
Row 3: Ch 1, turn; sc in first sc and in ea st across, change to MC in last st.
Row 4: With MC, ch 1, turn; sc in first sc, Ldc in 3rd sc from beg 3 rows below, * sk next sc on working row, sc in next sc, Ldc in same sc as prev Ldc [V-st made], sk next sc on working row **, sc in next 2 sc, Ldc in 4th sc from prev Ldc 3 rows below, sk next sc on working row, sc in next 2 sc, Ldc in 4th sc from prev Ldc 3 rows below; rep from * across, ending last rep at **, sc in last sc: 7 V-sts and 6 Ldc.
Row 5: Ch 1, turn; sc in first sc and in ea st across, change to CC in last st.
Row 6: With CC, ch 1, turn; sc in first 2 sc, Ldc in 3rd sc from beg 3 rows below, * sk next sc on working row, sc in next 2 sc **, FPdc around next Ldc 3 rows below, sk next sc on working row, sc in next sc, FPdc around same Ldc as last FPdc [V-st made], sk next sc on working row, sc in next 2 sc, Ldc in 4th sc from prev FPdc 3 rows below; rep from * across, ending last rep at **: 6 V-sts and 7 Ldc.
Row 7: Rep row 3.
Row 8: With MC, ch 1, turn; sc in first sc, * FPdc around next Ldc 3 rows below, sk next sc on working row, sc in next sc, FPdc around same Ldc as prev FPdc [V-st made], sk next sc on working row **, sc in next 2 sc, Ldc in 4th sc from prev FPdc 3 rows below, sk next sc on working row, sc in next 2 sc; rep from

* across, ending last rep at **, sc in last sc: 7 V-sts and 6 Ldc.
Rows 9–48: Rep rows 5–8, 10 times; do not turn after last row; fasten off CC; do not fasten off MC.

Border
Rnd 1 (rs): With rs facing and MC, ch 1, 3 sc in last st, sc evenly across to next corner, 3 sc in corner, sc in ea ch across to next corner, 3 sc in corner, sc evenly across to next corner, 3 sc in corner, sc in ea st across to next corner; join with sl st to beg sc; fasten off.
Rnd 2 (ws): With ws facing, join CC in any corner with sl st, ch 1, * 3 sc in corner, sc in ea sc across to next corner; rep from * around; join with sl st to beg sc; fasten off.
Rnd 3 (rs): With rs facing, join MC in top right corner with sl st, ch 1, working from left to right [reverse sc], sc in first sc and in ea sc around; join with sl st to beg sc; fasten off.

Project was stitched by Lily M. Chin with Kitchen Cotton: Morning Glory Blue #108 and Sunflower #157.

Gingham Checks

Cheerful checks add country comfort to any home. Worked in strips, this afghan requires less joining than individual squares would.

Materials
Worsted-weight wool-blend yarn, approximately:
21 oz. (1,380 yd.) cream, MC
21 oz. (1,380 yd.) green, CC
Size J crochet hook or size to obtain gauge
Yarn needle

Finished Size
Approximately 48" x 51"

Gauge
In pat, 9 sts and 11 rows = 3"

Gauge Swatch (Multiple of 4 sts + 2)
Work as for Strip A for 20 rows.

Pattern Stitch
Long double crochet [Ldc]: Yo, insert hook from front to back in st indicated, yo and pull up long lp, (yo and pull through 2 lps) twice.

Note: To change colors, work last yo of prev st with new color, dropping prev color to ws of work. Do not fasten off when changing colors.

Strip A (Make 4.)

*Color sequence: 1 row CC, * (2 rows MC, 2 rows CC) 7 times, fasten off MC, 24 rows CC; rep from * twice, (2 rows MC, 2 rows CC) 6 times, 2 rows MC, 1 row CC.*

With CC, ch 22 loosely.
Row 1 (ws): Sc in 2nd ch from hook and in ea ch across: 21 sc.

Row 2 (rs): Ch 1, turn; sc in first sc and in ea sc across.
Row 3 and all Odd Rows: Ch 1, turn; sc in first st and in ea st across.
Row 4: Ch 1, turn; sc in first sc, Ldc in 3rd sc from beg 3 rows below, * sk next sc on working row, sc in next sc, Ldc in same sc as prev Ldc 3 rows below [V-st made], sk next sc on working row, sc in next sc **, Ldc in 4th sc from prev Ldc 3 rows below; rep from * across, ending last rep at **: 5 V-sts.

Row 6: Ch 1, turn; sc in first 2 sc, Ldc in 3rd sc from beg 3 rows below [in center of V-st], * sk next sc on working row **, sc in next 3 sc, Ldc in 4th sc from prev Ldc 3 rows below [in center of V-st]; rep from * across, ending last rep at **, sc in last 2 sc: 5 Ldc.
Row 8: Ch 1, turn; sc in first 3 sc, Ldc in 5th sc from beg 3 rows below, * sk next sc on working

(Continued on page 48)

row, sc in next sc, Ldc in same sc as prev Ldc 3 rows below [V-st made], sk next sc on working row, sc in next sc **, Ldc in 4th sc from prev Ldc 3 rows below; rep from * across, ending last rep at **; sc in last 2 sc: 4 V-sts.

Row 10: Ch 1, turn; sc in first 4 sc, Ldc in 5th sc from beg 3 rows below [in center of V-st], * sk next sc on working row, sc in next 3 sc **, Ldc in 4th sc from prev Ldc 3 rows below [in center of V-st]; rep from * across, ending last rep at **, sc in last sc: 4 Ldc.

Rows 11–184: Rep rows 3–10, 21 times, then rep rows 3–8 once; fasten off after last row.

Strip B *(Make 3.)*

Color sequence: *28 rows MC, * (2 rows CC, 2 rows MC) 7 times, fasten off CC, 24 rows MC; rep from * twice.*

With MC, ch 22 loosely. Work pat same as Strip A, foll color sequence for Strip B.

Assembly

Beg and ending with Strip A, alternate strips and whipstitch strips tog.

Border

Rnd 1 (rs): With rs facing, join MC in top right corner with sl st, ch 1, 3 sc in corner, sc in ea st across to next corner, 3 sc in corner, sc evenly across to next corner, 3 sc in corner, sc in ea ch across to next corner, 3 sc in corner, sc evenly across to next corner; join with sl st to beg sc; fasten off.

Rnd 2 (ws): With ws facing, join CC in any corner with sl st, ch 1, * 3 sc in corner, sc in ea sc across to next corner; rep from * around; join with sl st to beg sc.

Rnd 3 (rs): Ch 1, turn; * sc in ea sc across to next corner, 3 sc in corner; rep from * around; join with sl st to beg sc; fasten off.

Project was stitched by Marge Wild with Wool-ease: Natural Heather #98 and Green Heather #130.

Mesh Stripes

Add a light airiness to a simple baby blanket with open mesh stripes. The border is also worked in the mesh pattern.

Materials

Sportweight acrylic yarn, approximately:
10½ oz. (1,180 yd.) white, MC
8¾ oz. (980 yd.) blue, A
7 oz. (785 yd.) lavender, B
Size H crochet hook or size to obtain gauge

Finished Size

Approximately 43" x 53"

Gauge

In pat, 14 sts and 20 rows = 4"

Gauge Swatch *(Multiple of 4 sts + 2)*

With MC, ch 22. Work in pat for 22 rows.

Pattern Stitches

Long double crochet [Ldc]: Yo, insert hook from front to back in st indicated, yo and pull up long lp, (yo and pull through 2 lps) twice.

Cluster [cl]: (Yo, insert hook in st indicated and pull up lp) twice, yo and pull through 4 lps on hook, yo and pull through 2 lps on hook.

Note: Afghan is worked sideways. To change colors, work last yo of prev st with new color, dropping prev color to ws of work. Do not fasten off when changing colors.

With MC, ch 182 loosely.

Row 1 (ws): Sc in 2nd ch from hook and in ea ch across, change to A in last st: 181 sc.

Row 2 (rs): With A, ch 1, turn; sc in first sc and in ea sc across.

Row 3: Ch 1, turn; sc in first sc and in ea st across, change to MC in last st.

Row 4: With MC, ch 1, turn; sc in first sc, Ldc in 2nd sc from beg 3 rows below, * sk next sc on working row, sc in next sc **, Ldc in 2nd sc from prev Ldc 3 rows below; rep from * across, ending last rep at **; change to B in last st: 90 Ldc.

Row 5: With B, ch 3, turn; cl in first sc, * ch 1, sk next st, cl in next st; rep from * across: 91 cl.

Row 6: Ch 3, turn; sk first cl, * cl in next ch-1 sp, ch 1, sk next cl; rep from * across, cl in last ch-3 sp; change to MC in last st; fasten off B: 91 cl.

Row 7: With MC, ch 1, turn; sc in first cl, sc in ea ch-1 sp and cl across, sk last ch-3 sp, change to A in last st: 181 sc.

Row 8: With A, ch 1, turn; sc in first sc and in ea sc across.

Row 9: Ch 1, turn; sc in first sc and in ea st across, change to MC in last st.

Row 10: With MC, rep row 4; do not change colors at end of row.

Row 11: Ch 1, turn; sc in first sc and in ea st across, change to A in last st.

Row 12: With A, ch 1, turn; sc in first 2 sc, Ldc in 3rd sc from beg 3 rows below, * sk next sc on working row **, sc in next sc, Ldc in 2nd sc from prev Ldc 3 rows below; rep from * across, ending last rep at **, sc in last 2 sc: 89 Ldc.

Rows 13–26: Rep rows 3–12 once, then rep rows 9–12 once.

Rows 27–44: Rep rows 3–12 once, then rep rows 9–12 twice.

Rows 45–66: Rep rows 3–12 once, then rep rows 9–12, 3 times.

Rows 67–92: Rep rows 3–12 once, then rep rows 9–12, 4 times.

Rows 93–114: Rep rows 3–12 once, then rep rows 9–12, 3 times.

Rows 115–132: Rep rows 3–12 once, then rep rows 9–12 twice.

Rows 133–146: Rep rows 3–12 once, then rep rows 9–12 once.

Rows 147–164: Rep rows 3–12 once, then rep rows 3–10 once; fasten off.

Border

Rnd 1 (rs): With rs facing, join B in top right corner with sl st, ch 1, sc in same st and in ea st across to next corner, 3 sc in corner, sc evenly across to next corner, 3 sc in corner, sc in ea ch across to next corner, 3 sc in corner, sc evenly across to next corner, 2 sc in corner; join with sl st to beg sc.

Rnd 2 (ws): Ch 3, turn; (cl, ch 1, cl) in corner st, (ch 1, sk next sc, cl in next sc) across to next corner, * (cl, ch 1, cl) in corner, (ch 1, sk next sc, cl in next sc) across to next corner; rep from * around, ch 1; join with sl st to top of beg ch-3.

Rnd 3 (rs): Ch 3, turn; * (cl in next ch-1 sp, ch 1) across to next corner ch-1 sp, (cl, ch 1, cl) in corner ch-1 sp; rep from * around, ch 1; join with sl st to top of beg ch-3; fasten off.

Project was stitched by Marge Scensny with Jamie Pompadour: White #200, Pastel Blue #206, and Lavender #244.

Greek Keys

Use a detail from ancient architecture to edge this classic afghan.

Materials

Worsted-weight wool-blend yarn, approximately:
42 oz. (2,760 yd.) gray, MC
12 oz. (790 yd.) red, CC
Size J crochet hook or size to obtain gauge

Finished Size

Approximately 53" x 57"

Gauge

In pat, 12 sts and 16 rows = 4"

Gauge Swatch *(Multiple of 6 sts + 4)*

With CC, ch 22. Work in pat for 20 rows.

Pattern Stitch

Long double crochet [Ldc]: Yo, insert hook from front to back in st indicated, yo and pull up long lp, (yo and pull through 2 lps) twice.

Note: To change colors, work last yo of prev st with new color, dropping prev color to ws of work. Do not fasten off when changing colors.

Color sequence: 1 row CC, (2 rows MC, 2 rows CC) 9 times, fasten off CC, 144 rows MC, (2 rows CC, 2 rows MC) 9 times, 2 rows CC, 1 row MC.

With CC, ch 154 loosely.

Row 1 (ws): Sc in 2nd ch from hook and in ea ch across: 153 sc.

Row 2 (rs): Ch 1, turn; sc in first sc and in ea sc across.

Row 3 and all Odd Rows: Ch 1, turn; sc in first sc and in ea st across.

Row 4: Ch 1, turn; sc in first sc, Ldc in 2nd sc from beg 3 rows below, * sk next sc on working row **, sc in next 5 sc, Ldc in 6th sc from prev Ldc 3 rows below; rep from * across, ending last rep at **, sc in last sc: 26 Ldc.

Row 6: Ch 1, turn; sc in first 2 sc, Ldc in 3rd sc from beg 3 rows below, * sk next sc on working row, sc in next 3 sc, Ldc in 4th sc from prev Ldc 3 rows below, sk next sc on working row, sc in next sc **, Ldc in 2nd sc from prev Ldc 3 rows below; rep from * across, ending last rep at **, sc in last sc: 50 Ldc.

Row 8: Ch 1, turn; sc in first sc, Ldc in 2nd sc from beg 3 rows below, * sk next sc on working row, sc in next sc **, Ldc in 2nd sc from prev Ldc 3 rows below; rep from * across, ending last rep at **: 76 Ldc.

(Continued on page 54)

Row 10: Ch 1, turn; sc in first 2 sc, Ldc in 3rd sc from beg 3 rows below, * sk next sc on working row, sc in next sc **, Ldc in 2nd sc from prev Ldc 3 rows below; rep from * across, ending last rep at **, sc in last sc: 75 Ldc.

Row 12: Ch 1, turn; sc in first 3 sc, Ldc in 4th sc from beg 3 rows below, * sk next sc on working row, sc in next sc, Ldc in 2nd sc from prev Ldc 3 rows below, sk next sc on working row, sc in next 3 sc **, Ldc in 4th sc from prev Ldc 3 rows below; rep from * across, ending last rep at **: 50 Ldc.

Row 14: Ch 1, turn; sc in first 4 sc, Ldc in 5th sc from beg 3 rows below, * sk next sc on working row **, sc in next 5 sc, Ldc in 6th sc from prev Ldc 3 rows below; rep from * across, ending last rep at **, sc in last 4 sc: 25 Ldc.

Rows 15–220: Rep rows 3–14, 17 times, then rep rows 3 and 4 once; fasten off after last row.

Border

Rnd 1 (rs): With rs facing, join MC in top right corner with sl st, ch 1, 3 sc in corner, sc in ea st across to next corner, 3 sc in corner, sc evenly across to next corner, 3 sc in corner, sc in ea ch across to next corner, 3 sc in corner, sc evenly across to next corner; join with sl st to beg sc; fasten off.

Rnd 2 (ws): With ws facing, join CC in any corner with sl st, ch 1, * sc in ea sc across to next corner, 3 sc in corner; rep from * around; join with sl st to beg sc.

Rnd 3 (rs): Ch 1, turn; * sc in ea sc across to next corner, 3 sc in corner; rep from * around; join with sl st to beg sc.

Rnd 4 (rs): Sl st in same st and in ea sc around; join with sl st to beg sl st; fasten off.

Project was stitched by Joann Moss with Wool-ease: Grey Heather #151 and Cranberry #138.

Colorful Crayons

Stripes of bold colors are as inviting as a new box of crayons. The pattern stitch looks different on both sides, making this a fully reversible afghan.

Materials

Worsted-weight acrylic yarn, approximately:
36 oz. (1,800 yd.) white, MC
12 oz. (600 yd.) purple, A
12 oz. (600 yd.) yellow, B
12 oz. (600 yd.) green, C
12 oz. (600 yd.) red, D
12 oz. (600 yd.) blue, E
Size K crochet hook or size to obtain gauge

Finished Size

Approximately 53" x 64", without fringe

Gauge

In pat, 11 sts and 14 rows = 4"

Gauge Swatch *(Multiple of 6 sts)*

Work as for Strip for 16 rows.

Pattern Stitches

Long double crochet [Ldc]: Yo, insert hook from front to back in st indicated, yo and pull up long lp, (yo and pull through 2 lps) twice.

Front Post treble crochet [FPtr]: Yo twice, insert hook from front to back around post of st indicated, yo and pull up lp, (yo and pull through 2 lps) 3 times.

Note: *To change colors, work last yo of prev st with new color, dropping prev color to ws of work. Do not fasten off when changing colors.*

Strip *(Make 1 ea with A as CC, B as CC, C as CC, D as CC, and E as CC.)*

With CC, ch 30 loosely.

Row 1 (ws): Sc in 2nd ch from hook and in ea ch across, change to MC in last st: 29 sc.

Row 2 (rs): With MC, ch 1, turn; sc in first sc and in ea sc across.

Row 3: Ch 1, turn; sc in first sc and in ea st across, change to CC in last st.

Row 4: With CC, ch 1, turn; sc in first sc, Ldc in 3rd sc from beg 3 rows below, * sk next sc on working row, sc in next sc, Ldc in same sc as prev Ldc [V-st made], sk next sc on working row, sc in next sc **, Ldc in 3rd sc from prev Ldc 3 rows below, sk next sc on working row, sc in next sc, Ldc in 3rd sc from prev Ldc 3 rows below; rep from * across, ending last rep at **: 5 V-sts and 4 Ldc.

Row 5: Ch 1, turn; sc in first sc and in ea st across, change to MC in last st.

Row 6: With MC, ch 1, turn; sc in first 2 sc, Ldc in 3rd sc from beg 3 rows below, * sk next sc on working row, sc in next sc **, FPtr around next Ldc 3 rows below, sk next sc on working row, sc in next sc, FPtr around same Ldc as last FPtr [V-st made], sk next sc on working row, sc in next sc, Ldc in 3rd sc from prev FPtr 3 rows below; rep from * across, ending last rep at **, sc in last sc: 4 V-sts and 5 Ldc.

Row 7: Rep row 3.

Row 8: With CC, ch 1, turn; sc in first sc, FPtr around next Ldc 3 rows below, * sk next sc on working row, sc in next sc, FPtr around same Ldc as prev FPtr [V-st made], sk next sc on working row, sc in next sc **, Ldc in 3rd sc from prev FPtr 3 rows below, sk next sc on working row, sc in next sc, FPtr around next Ldc 3 rows below; rep from * across, ending last rep at **: 5 V-sts and 4 Ldc.
Rows 9–224: Rep rows 5–8, 54 times; fasten off.

Assembly
With MC, join strips tog with sc.

Border
With rs facing, join MC in any corner with sl st, ch 1, * sc evenly across to next corner, 3 sc in corner; rep from * around; join with sl st to beg sc; fasten off.

Fringe
For ea tassel, referring to page 143 of General Directions, cut 2 (12") lengths of yarn. Working across short ends, knot 1 tassel in ea st, matching colors with ea strip and alternating CC and MC.

Project was stitched by Margarete Dahlke with Jamie 4-ply: White #100, Purple #147, Buttercup #158, Evergreen #130, Red #133, and Blue #109.

Corn Silks

*Soft green yarn surrounds a golden field. Finish this throw
with an easy shell-stitch border.*

Materials

Worsted-weight mohair-blend
yarn, approximately:
30 oz. (2,665 yd.) yellow, MC
10 oz. (890 yd.) green, CC
Size I crochet hook or size to
obtain gauge
Yarn needle

Finished Size

Approximately 53" x 63"

Gauge

In pat, 12 sts and 16 rows = 4"

Gauge Swatch *(Multiple of 6 sts + 4)*

With CC, ch 22.
Work as for Center Panel for
25 rows.

Pattern Stitch

Long double crochet [Ldc]: Yo,
insert hook from front to back in st
indicated, yo and pull up long lp,
(yo and pull through 2 lps) twice.

Note: *To change colors, work
last yo of prev st with new color,
dropping prev color to ws of
work. Do not fasten off when
changing colors.*

Center Panel *(Make 1.)*

With CC, ch 118 loosely.
Row 1 (ws): Sc in 2nd ch from
hook and in ea ch across, change
to MC in last st: 117 sc.
Row 2 (rs): With MC, ch 1, turn;
sc in first sc and in ea sc across.
Row 3: Ch 1, turn; sc in first sc
and in ea st across, change to CC
in last st.

Row 4: With CC, ch 1, turn; sc in
first 3 sc, Ldc in 5th sc from beg
3 rows below, * sk next sc on
working row, sc in next sc, Ldc in
same sc as prev Ldc 3 rows below
[V-st made], sk next sc on working row, sc in next 3 sc **, Ldc in
6th sc from prev Ldc 3 rows
below; rep from * across, ending
last rep at **: 19 V-sts.
Row 5: Ch 1, turn; sc in first sc
and in ea st across, change to MC
in last st; ch 1, turn.
Row 6: With MC, sc in first sc,
Ldc in 3rd sc from beg 3 rows
below, * sk next sc on working
row, sc in next sc, Ldc in same sc
as prev Ldc 3 rows below [V-st
made], sk next sc on working
row, sc in next 3 sc **, Ldc in 6th
sc from prev Ldc 3 rows below;
rep from * across, ending last rep
at **; sc in last 2 sc: 19 V-sts.
Row 7: Rep row 3.
Row 8: With CC, ch 1, turn; sc in
first 5 sc, Ldc in 7th sc from beg
3 rows below, * sk next sc on
working row, sc in next sc, Ldc in
same sc as prev Ldc 3 rows below
[V-st made], sk next sc on working row **, sc in next 3 sc, Ldc in
6th sc from prev Ldc 3 rows
below; rep from * across, ending
last rep at **; sc in last sc:
19 V-sts.
Row 9: Rep row 5.
Row 10: With MC, rep row 4.
Row 11: Rep row 3.
Row 12: With CC, rep row 6.
Row 13: Rep row 5.
Row 14: With MC, rep row 8.
Rows 15–26: Rep rows 3–14
once; fasten of CC.
Rows 27–226: With MC and
without changing colors, rep rows

3–14, 16 times, then rep rows
3–10 once.
Rows 227–252: Changing colors
as specified, rep rows 11–14
once, then rep rows 3–14 once,
then rep rows 3–12 once; fasten
off.

Side Panel *(Make 2.)*

With CC, ch 22 loosely.
Row 1 (ws): Sc in 2nd ch from
hook and in ea ch across, change
to MC in last st: 21 sc.
Row 2 (rs): With MC, ch 1, turn;
sc in first sc and in ea sc across.
Rows 3–252: Rep rows 3–14 of
Center Panel, 20 times, then rep
rows 3–12 once; fasten off.

Assembly

Whipstitch 1 Side Panel to ea side
of Center Panel.

Border

Rnd 1 (rs): With rs facing, join
CC in top right corner with sl st,
ch 1, 3 sc in corner, work 153 sc
evenly across to next corner,
3 sc in corner, work 185 sc evenly
across to next corner, 3 sc in
corner, work 153 sc evenly across
to next corner, 3 sc in corner,
work 185 sc evenly across to next
corner; join with sl st to beg sc:
688 sc.
Rnd 2 (ws): Ch 1, turn; * sc in
ea sc across to corner, 3 sc in
corner; rep from * around; join
with sl st to beg sc; fasten off.
Rnd 3 (rs): Join MC in top right
corner with sl st, ch 1, sc in same
st, * sk next 2 sc, 5 dc in next
sc **, sk next 2 sc, sc in next sc;

(Continued on page 60)

rep from * around, ending last
rep at **, join with sl st to beg sc;
fasten off.

*Project was stitched by Madeline
Speziale with Imagine: Maize #186 and
Pine #173.*

Burgundy Blues

Chunky textured yarn works up quickly. Choose two tones of each color to create both vertical and horizontal stripes.

Materials
Chunky-weight acrylic bouclé
yarn, approximately:
24 oz. (740 yd.) dark blue, MC
24 oz. (740 yd.) light blue, A
24 oz. (740 yd.) burgundy, B
24 oz. (740 yd.) rose, C
Size K crochet hook or size to
obtain gauge

Finished Size
Approximately 54" x 67"

Gauge
In pat, 9 sts and 10½ rows = 4"

Gauge Swatch *(Multiple of 6 sts + 4)*
With MC, ch 22. Work in pat for
16 rows.

Pattern Stitch
Long double crochet [Ldc]: Yo,
insert hook from front to back in
st indicated, yo and pull up long
lp, (yo and pull through 2 lps)
twice.

Note: *To change colors, work
last yo of prev st with new color,
dropping prev color to ws of
work. Do not fasten off when
changing colors.*

*Color sequence: 1 row MC,
(2 rows A, 2 rows MC) 5 times,
2 rows C, 2 rows B, 2 rows C,
fasten off B and C, (2 rows MC,
2 rows A) 5 times, 2 rows MC,
fasten off MC and A, (2 rows C,
2 rows B) 7 times, 2 rows C,
fasten off B and C, (2 rows MC,
2 rows A) 3 times, 2 rows MC,
fasten off MC and A, (2 rows C,
2 rows B) 7 times, 2 rows C,
fasten off B and C, (2 rows MC,
2 rows A), 5 times, 2 rows MC,
2 rows C, 2 rows B, 2 rows C,
fasten off B and C, (2 rows MC,
2 rows A) 5 times, 1 row MC.*

With MC, ch 118 loosely.

Row 1 [ws]: Sc in 2nd ch from hook and in ea ch across: 117 sc.

Row 2 [rs]: Ch 1, turn; sc in first sc and in ea sc across.

Row 3 and all Odd Rows: Ch 1, turn; sc in first sc and in ea st across.

Row 4: Ch 1, turn; sc in first 2 sc, Ldc in 5th sc from beg 3 rows below, * (sk next sc on working row, sc in next sc, Ldc in same sc as prev Ldc 3 rows below) twice, sk next sc on working row, sc in next sc [shell st made] **, Ldc in 6th sc from prev Ldc 3 rows below; rep from * across, ending last rep at **, sc in last sc: 19 shell sts.

Row 6: Ch 1, turn; sc in first sc, Ldc in 2nd sc from beg 3 rows below, sk next sc on working row, sc in next sc, Ldc in same sc as prev Ldc 3 rows below, sk next sc on working row, sc in next sc [half shell st made], * Ldc in 6th sc from prev Ldc 3 rows below **, (sk next sc on working row, sc in next sc, Ldc in same sc as prev Ldc 3 rows below) twice, sk next sc on working row, sc in next sc [shell st made]; rep from * across, ending last rep at **, sk next sc on working row, sc in next sc, Ldc in same sc as prev Ldc, sk next sc on working row, sc in last sc [half shell st made]: 18 shell sts and 2 half shell sts.

Rows 7–172: Rep rows 3–6, 41 times, then rep rows 3 and 4 once; fasten off.

Border

Rnd 1 [rs]: With rs facing, join C in top right corner with sl st, ch 1, 3 sc in corner, sc in ea st across to next corner, 3 sc in corner, sc evenly across to next corner, 3 sc in corner, sc in ea ch across to next corner, 3 sc in corner, sc evenly across to next corner; join with sl st to beg sc.

Rnd 2 [ws]: Ch 1, turn; * sc in ea sc across to next corner, 3 sc in corner; rep from * around; join with sl st to beg sc; fasten off.

Rnd 3 [rs]: With rs facing, join B in any corner with sl st, ch 1, * 3 sc in corner, sc in ea sc across to next corner; rep from * around; join with sl st to beg sc.

Rnd 4 [rs]: Ch 1, working from left to right [reverse sc], sc in same sc and in ea sc around; join with sl st to beg sc; fasten off.

Project was stitched by Margarete Dahlke with Homespun: Colonial #302, Williamsburg #321, Antique #307, and Baroque #322.

Warm Woods

Slanted stitches in rich browns branch out like trees against a blustery sky. Cuddle up in this thick throw after a walk on a chilly autumn evening.

Materials

Super chunky-weight wool-blend yarn, approximately:
48 oz. (865 yd.) brown, MC
48 oz. (865 yd.) cream, CC
Size Q crochet hook or size to obtain gauge

Finished Size

Approximately 55" x 68"

Gauge

In pat, 4½ sts and 6 rows = 4"

Gauge Swatch *(Multiple of 16 sts + 10)*

With MC, ch 26. Work in pat for 8 rows.

Pattern Stitch

Long double crochet [Ldc]: Yo, insert hook from front to back in st indicated, yo and pull up long lp, (yo and pull through 2 lps) twice.

Note: To change colors, work last yo of prev st with new color, dropping prev color to ws of work. Do not fasten off when changing colors.

With MC, ch 58 loosely.

Row 1 (ws): Sc in 2nd ch from hook and in ea ch across, change to CC in last st: 57 sc.

Row 2 (rs): With CC, ch 1, turn; sc in first sc and in ea sc across.

Row 3: Ch 1, turn; sc in first sc and in ea st across, change to MC in last st.

Row 4: With MC, ch 1, turn; sc in first sc, Ldc in 4th sc from beg 3 rows below [slant-st made], * sk next sc on working row, sc in next sc, Ldc in same sc as prev Ldc 3 rows below, sk next sc on working row, sc in next sc, Ldc in 2nd sc from prev Ldc 3 rows below, sk next sc on working row, sc in next sc, Ldc in same sc as prev Ldc [slant-st made], sk next sc on working row **, sc in next 2 sc, Ldc in 5th sc from prev Ldc 3 rows below [slant-st made], (sk next sc on working row, sc in next sc, Ldc in 2nd sc from prev Ldc 3 rows below) twice, sk next sc on working row, sc in next 2 sc, Ldc in 5th sc from prev Ldc 3 rows below [slant-st made]; rep from * across, ending last rep at **, sc in last sc: 17 Ldc and 8 slant-sts.

Row 5: Ch 1, turn; sc in first sc and in ea st across, change to CC in last st.

Row 6: With CC, ch 1, turn; sc in first 2 sc, Ldc in 3rd sc from beg 3 rows below, * (sk next sc on working row, sc in next sc, Ldc in 2nd sc from prev Ldc 3 rows below) twice, sk next sc on working row, sc in next 2 sc **, Ldc in 5th sc from prev Ldc 3 rows below [slant-st made], sk next sc on working row, sc in next sc, Ldc in same sc as prev Ldc 3 rows below, sk next sc on working row, sc in next sc, Ldc in 2nd sc from prev Ldc 3 rows below, sk next sc on working row, sc in next sc, Ldc in same sc as prev Ldc 3 rows below [slant-st made], sk next sc on working row, sc in next 2 sc, Ldc in 5th sc from prev Ldc 3 rows below; rep from * across, ending last rep at **: 18 Ldc and 6 slant-sts.

Rows 7–96: Rep rows 3–6, 22 times, then rep rows 3 and 4 once; do not turn after last row; fasten off CC; do not fasten off MC.

Border

Rnd 1 (rs): With rs facing and MC, ch 1, 3 sc in last st, sc evenly across to next corner, 3 sc in corner, sc in ea ch across to next corner, 3 sc in corner, sc evenly across to next corner, 3 sc in corner, sc in ea st across to next corner; join with sl st to beg sc; fasten off.

Rnd 2 (ws): With ws facing join CC in any corner with sl st, ch 1, * sc in ea sc across to next corner, 3 sc in corner; rep from * around; join with sl st to beg sc.

Rnd 3 (rs): Ch 1, turn; * sc in ea sc across to next corner, 3 sc in corner; rep from * around; join with sl st to beg sc; fasten off.

Rnd 4 (rs): With rs facing, join MC in any corner with sl st, ch 1, working from left to right [reverse sc], sc in first sc and in ea sc around; join with sl st to beg sc; fasten off.

Project was stitched by Madeline Speziale with Wool-ease Thick & Quick: Wood #404 and Wheat #402.

Quilted Trellis

Create this striking diamond pattern with easy post stitches. A second pattern develops on the reverse side.

Materials
Chunky-weight acrylic bouclé
  yarn, approximately:
36 oz. (1,110 yd.) gray-and-
  green variegated, MC
Chunky-weight brushed
  acrylic yarn, approximately:
30 oz. (1,350 yd.) teal, CC
Size K crochet hook or size to
  obtain gauge

Finished Size
Approximately 50" x 56"

Gauge
In pat, 10 sts and 11 rows = 4"

Gauge Swatch *(Multiple of 6 sts + 3)*

Front

Back

With CC, ch 21. Work in pat for
18 rows.

Pattern Stitches
**Front Post treble crochet
[FPtr]:** Yo twice, insert hook
from front to back around post of
st indicated, yo and pull up lp,
(yo and pull through 2 lps) 3 times.
Long double crochet [Ldc]: Yo,
insert hook from front to back in st
indicated, yo and pull up long lp,
(yo and pull through 2 lps) twice.

Note: *To change colors, work
last yo of prev st with new color,
dropping prev color to ws of
work. Do not fasten off when
changing colors.*

With CC, ch 123 loosely.
Row 1 (ws): Sc in 2nd ch from
hook and in ea ch across, change
to MC in last st: 122 sc.
Row 2 (rs): With MC, ch 1, turn;
sc in first sc and in ea sc across.
Row 3: Ch 1, turn; sc in first sc
and in ea st across, change to CC
in last st.
Row 4: With CC, ch 1, turn; sc in
first sc, FPtr around 5th sc from
beg 3 rows below [slant-st made],
sk next sc on working row, * sc in
next 4 sc, FPtr around first sc
after prev FPtr 3 rows below
[slant-st made] **, sk 4 sc 3 rows
below, FPtr around next sc 3
rows below [slant-st made],
sk next 2 sc on working row; rep
from * across, ending last rep
at **; sk next sc on working row,
sc in last sc: 40 slant-sts.
Row 5: Ch 1, turn; sc in first sc
and in ea st across, change to MC
in last st.

Row 6: With MC, ch 1, turn; sc in
first 2 sc, * Ldc in next sc 3 rows
below, sk next sc on working row,
sc in next 2 sc; rep from * across:
40 Ldc.
Row 7: Rep row 3.
Row 8: With CC, ch 1, turn; sc in
first 3 sc, FPtr around 3rd sc
from beg 3 rows below [slant-st
made], * sk next 4 sc 3 rows
below, FPtr around next sc 3
rows below [slant-st made],
sk next 2 sc on working row **,
sc in next 4 sc, FPtr around first
sc after prev FPtr 3 rows below
[slant-st made]; rep from * across,
ending last rep at **, sc in last
3 sc: 40 slant-sts.
Rows 9 and 10: Rep rows 5 and
6 once.
Rows 11–152: Rep rows 3–10,
17 times, then rep rows 3–8 once;
do not turn after last row; fasten
of MC; do not fasten off CC.

Border
Rnd 1 (rs): With rs facing and
CC, ch 1, 3 sc in last st, work 145
sc evenly across to next corner,
3 sc in corner, sc in ea ch across
to next corner [122 sc], 3 sc in
corner, work 145 sc evenly across
to next corner, 3 sc in corner,
sc in ea st across to next corner
[122 sc]; join with sl st to beg sc:
546 sc.
Rnd 2 (rs): Sl st in first 2 sc,
* (sl st, ch 3, sl st) in next sc
[picot made] **, sl st in next 2 sc;
rep from * around, ending last rep
at **, sl st to beg sl st; fasten off.

*Project was stitched by Peggy Stiver
with Homespun: Regency #320 and
Jiffy: Teal #178.*

Checkerboard Squares

Make this afghan on the go, with its small, portable blocks. Match the colors to your favorite team for a super stadium blanket.

Materials
Worsted-weight wool-blend yarn, approximately:
30 oz. (1,970 yd.) cream, MC
15 oz. (985 yd.) dark green, A
15 oz. (985 yd.) burgundy, B
Size J crochet hook or size to obtain gauge
Yarn needle

Finished Size
Approximately 53" x 68"

Gauge
Ea Block = 7½"

Gauge Swatch *(Multiple of 4 sts)*
Work as for Block 1.

Note: Gauge is crucial when pieces are sewn together, especially when they are turned sideways.

Pattern Stitch
Long double crochet [Ldc]: Yo, insert hook from front to back in st indicated, yo and pull up long lp, (yo and pull through 2 lps) twice.

Note: To change colors, work last yo of prev st with new color, dropping prev color to ws of work. Do not fasten off when changing colors.

Block 1 *(Make 32.)*
With A, ch 24 loosely.
Row 1 (ws): Sc in 2nd ch from hook and in each ch across; change to MC: 23 sts.
Row 2 (rs): With MC, ch 1, turn; sc in first sc and in ea sc across.
Row 3: Ch 1, turn; sc in first sc and in ea st across; change to A in last st.
Row 4: With A, ch 1, turn; sc in first 3 sc, * Ldc in next sc 3 rows below, sk next sc on working row, sc in next 3 sc; rep from * across: 5 Ldc.
Row 5: Ch 1, turn; sc in first sc and in ea st across, change to MC in last st.
Row 6: With MC, ch 1, turn; sc in first sc, * Ldc in next sc 3 rows below, sk next sc on working row **, sc in next 3 sc; rep from * across, ending last rep at **, sc in last sc: 6 Ldc.
Rows 7–28: Rep rows 3–6, 5 times, then rep rows 3 and 4 once; fasten off.

Block 2 *(Make 31.)*
With B, ch 24 loosely.
Row 1 (ws): Sc in 2nd ch from hook and in each ch across;

change to MC in last st: 23 sts.
Row 2 (rs): With MC, ch 1, turn; sc in first sc and in ea sc across.
Row 3: Ch 1, turn; sc in first sc and in ea st across, change to B in last st.
Row 4: With B, ch 1, turn; sc in first sc, * Ldc in next sc 3 rows below, sk next sc on working row **, sc in next 3 sc; rep from * across, ending last rep at **, sc in last sc: 6 Ldc.
Row 5: Ch 1, turn; sc in first sc and in ea st across, change to MC in last st.
Row 6: With MC, ch 1, turn; sc in first 3 sc, * Ldc over next sc, sc in next 3 sc; rep from * across: 5 Ldc.
Rows 7–28: Rep rows 3–6, 5 times, then rep rows 3 and 4 once; fasten off.

Assembly
Afghan is 7 blocks wide and 9 blocks long. Alternate blocks to form checkerboard pattern, turning all Block 2s sideways. Whipstitch blocks tog.

Border
Rnd 1 (rs): With rs facing, join MC in any corner with sl st; ch 1, * 3 sc in corner, sc evenly across to next corner; rep from * around; join with sl st to beg sc.
Rnd 2 (rs): Working from left to right [reverse sc], ch 1, sc in first sc and in ea sc around; join with sl st to beg sc; fasten off.

Project was stitched by Margarete Dahlke with Wool-ease: Ivory Sprinkles #97, Hunter Green Sprinkles #131, and Burgundy Sprinkles #142.

Rustic Rug and Pillow

Crochet a sturdy rug from extrathick yarn. Then compliment the look with a matching tasseled pillow.

Rug

Materials
Super chunky-weight wool-blend yarn, approximately:
42 oz. (760 yd.) burgundy, MC
30 oz. (540 yd.) gray, CC
Size N crochet hook or size to obtain gauge

Finished Size
Approximately 34" x 56", without fringe

Gauge
In pat, 6 sts and 8 rows = 4"

Gauge Swatch *(Multiple of 14 sts + 8)*
With MC, ch 22. Work in pat for 14 rows.

Pattern Stitch
Long double crochet [Ldc]: Yo, insert hook from front to back in st indicated, yo and pull up long lp, (yo and pull through 2 lps) twice.

Note: To change colors, work last yo of prev st with new color, dropping prev color to ws of work. Do not fasten off when changing colors.

Rug
With MC, ch 50 loosely.
Row 1 (ws): Sc in 2nd ch from hook and in ea ch across, change to CC in last st: 49 sc.
Row 2 (rs): With CC, ch 1, turn; sc in first sc and in ea sc across.
Row 3: Ch 1, turn; sc in first sc and in ea st across, change to MC in last st.
Row 4: With MC, ch 1, turn; sc in first 2 sc, Ldc in 3rd sc from beg 3 rows below, * sk next sc on working row, sc in next sc, Ldc in 2nd sc from prev Ldc 3 rows below, sk next sc on working row **, sc in next 11 sc, Ldc in 12th sc from prev Ldc 3 rows below; rep from * across, ending last rep at **; sc in last 2 sc: 8 Ldc.
Row 5: Ch 1, turn; sc in first sc and in ea st across, change to CC in last st.
Row 6: With CC, ch 1, turn; sc in first sc, Ldc in 2nd sc from beg 3 rows below, * (sk next sc on working row, sc in next sc, Ldc in 2nd sc from prev Ldc 3 rows below) twice, sk next sc on working row **, sc in next 9 sc, Ldc in 10th sc from prev Ldc 3 rows below; rep from * across, ending last rep at **; sc in last sc: 12 Ldc.
Row 7: Rep row 3.
Row 8: With MC, ch 1, turn; sc in first 6 sc, Ldc in 7th sc from beg 3 rows below, * (sk next sc on working row, sc in next sc, Ldc in 2nd sc from prev Ldc 3 rows below) 4 times, sk next sc on working row, sc in next 5 sc **, Ldc in 6th sc from prev Ldc 3 rows below; rep from * across, ending last rep at **; sc in last sc: 15 Ldc.
Row 9: Rep row 5.
Row 10: With CC, ch 1, turn; sc in first 7 sc, Ldc in 8th sc from beg 3 rows below, * (sk next sc on working row, sc in next sc, Ldc in 2nd sc from prev Ldc 3 rows below) 3 times, sk next sc on working row, sc in next 7 sc **, Ldc in 8th sc from prev Ldc 3 rows below; rep from * across, ending last rep at **: 12 Ldc.
Row 11: Rep row 3.
Row 12: Rep row 8.
Row 13: Rep row 5.
Row 14: Rep row 6.
Rows 15–112: Rep rows 3–14, 8 times, then rep rows 3 and 4 once; do not turn after last row; fasten off CC; do not fasten off MC.

Border
Rnd 1 (rs): With rs facing and MC, ch 1, 3 sc in last st, sc evenly across to next corner, 3 sc in corner, sc in ea ch across to next corner, 3 sc in corner, sc evenly across to next corner, 3 sc in corner, sc in ea st across to next corner; join with sl st to beg sc.
Rnd 2 (ws): Turn; sl st in same st and in ea st around; join with sl st to beg sl st; fasten off.

Fringe
For ea tassel, referring to page 143 of General Directions, cut 3 (16") lengths of CC. Working across short ends, knot 1 tassel in every other st.

Project was stitched by Madeline Speziale with Wool-ease Thick & Quick: Claret #143 and Pewter #152.

(Continued on page 72)

Pillow

Materials

Worsted-weight wool-blend yarn, approximately:
6 oz. (395 yd.) burgundy, MC
6 oz. (395 yd.) gray, CC
Size F crochet hook or size to obtain gauge
12" pillow form
Yarn needle

Finished Size

Approximately 12"

Gauge

In pat, 17 sts and 21 rows = 4"

Gauge Swatch (Multiple of 14 sts + 8)

With MC, ch 22. Work in pat for 22 rows.

Pattern Stitch

Long double crochet [Ldc]: Yo, insert hook from front to back in st indicated, yo and pull up long lp, (yo and pull through 2 lps) twice.

Note: To change colors, work last yo of prev st with new color, dropping prev color to ws of work. Do not fasten off when changing colors.

Pillow Front

With MC, ch 50 loosely.
Work as for Rug for 64 rows.
Border
With rs facing and MC, ch 1, 3 sc in last st, work 47 sc evenly across to next corner, 3 sc in corner, sc in ea ch across to next corner [47 sc], 3 sc in corner, work 47 sc evenly across to next corner, 3 sc in corner, sc in ea st across to next corner [47 sc]; join with sl st to beg sc; fasten off.

Pillow Back

Work as for Pillow Front; do not fasten off after rnd 1 of Border.

Assembly

With ws facing and MC, join Pillow Back to Pillow Front with sl st in ea st around, slipping pillow form inside before finishing joining; join with sl st to beg sl st; fasten off.

Tassels

For ea tassel, referring to page 143 of General Directions, wind yarn around 8" piece of cardboard 60 times. Join 1 tassel to ea corner of Pillow.

Project was stitched by Madeline Speziale with Wool-ease: Chestnut Heather #179 and Grey Heather #151.

Bramble Berries

Sumptuous chenille yarn gives this afghan a lush texture. Combine the deep berry color with a lighter yarn for strong contrast.

Materials

Worsted-weight chenille yarn, approximately:

22½ oz. (1,395 yd.) burgundy, MC

21 oz. (1,305 yd.) tan, CC

Size G crochet hook or size to obtain gauge

Finished Size

Approximately 43" x 48"

Gauge

In pat, 14 sts and 17 rows = 4"

Gauge Swatch *(Multiple of 12 sts)*

WIth CC, ch 24. Work in pat for 20 rows.

Pattern Stitch

Long double crochet [Ldc]: Yo, insert hook from front to back in st indicated, yo and pull up long lp, (yo and pull through 2 lps) twice.

Note: To change colors, work last yo of prev st with new color, dropping prev color to ws of work. Do not fasten off when changing colors.

With MC, ch 144 loosely.

Row 1 (ws): Sc in 2nd ch from hook and in ea ch across, change to CC in last st: 143 sc.

Row 2 (rs): With CC, ch 1, turn; sc in first sc and in ea sc across.

Row 3: Ch 1, turn; sc in first sc and in ea st across, change to MC in last st.

Row 4: With MC, ch 1, turn; sc in first sc, Ldc in 4th sc from beg 3 rows below [slant-st made], * sk next sc on working row, sc in next sc, Ldc in same sc as prev Ldc 3 rows below, sk next sc on working row, sc in next sc, (Ldc in 2nd sc from prev Ldc 3 rows below, sk next sc on working row, sc in next sc) twice, Ldc in same sc as prev Ldc 3 rows below [slant-st made], sk next sc on working row, sc in next sc **, Ldc in 4th sc from prev Ldc 3 rows below, sk next sc on working row, sc in next sc, Ldc in 4th sc from prev Ldc 3 rows below [slant-st made]; rep from * across, ending last rep at **: 24 slant-sts and 47 Ldc.

Row 5: Ch 1, turn; sc in first sc and in ea st across, change to CC in last st.

Row 6: With CC, ch 1, turn; sc in first 2 sc, Ldc in 5th sc from beg 3 rows below [slant-st made], * sk next sc on working row, sc in next sc, Ldc in same sc as prev Ldc 3 rows below, sk next sc on working row, sc in next sc, Ldc in 2nd sc from prev Ldc 3 rows below, sk next sc on working row, sc in next sc, Ldc in same sc as prev Ldc 3 rows below [slant-st made], sk next sc on working row, sc in next sc **, Ldc in 4th sc from prev Ldc 3 rows below, sk next sc on working row, sc in next sc, Ldc in 2nd sc from prev Ldc 3 rows below, sk next sc on working row, sc in next sc, Ldc in

4th sc from prev Ldc 3 rows below [slant-st made]; rep from * across, ending last rep at **; sc in last sc: 24 slant-sts and 46 Ldc.

Row 7: Rep row 3.

Row 8: With MC, ch 1, turn; sc in first sc, Ldc in 2nd sc from beg 3 rows below, * sk next sc on working row, sc in next sc, Ldc in same sc as prev Ldc 3 rows below [slant-st made], sk next sc on working row, sc in next sc, (Ldc in 4th sc from prev Ldc 3 rows below, sk next sc on working row, sc in next sc) twice, Ldc in same sc as prev Ldc 3 rows below, sk next sc on working row, sc in next sc **, Ldc in 2nd sc from prev Ldc 3 rows below, sk next sc on working row, sc in next sc, Ldc in 2nd sc from prev Ldc 3 rows below; rep from * across, ending last rep at **: 24 slant-sts and 47 Ldc.

Row 9: Rep row 5.

Row 10: With CC, ch 1, turn; sc in first 4 sc, Ldc in 5th sc from beg 3 rows below, * sk next sc on working row, sc in next sc, Ldc in 2nd sc from prev Ldc 3 rows below, sk next sc on working row, sc in next sc **, Ldc in 4th sc from prev Ldc 3 rows below [slant-st made], sk next sc on working row, sc in next sc, Ldc in same sc as prev Ldc 3 rows below, sk next sc on working row, sc in next sc, Ldc in 2nd sc from prev Ldc 3 rows below, sk next sc on working row, sc in next sc, Ldc in same sc as prev Ldc 3 rows below [slant-st made], sk next sc on working row, sc in next sc, Ldc in 4th sc from prev Ldc 3 rows below; rep from * across, ending last rep at **; sc in last 3 sc: 22 slant-sts and 46 Ldc.

Rows 11–196: Rep rows 3–10, 23 times, then rep rows 3 and 4 once; do not turn after last row; fasten off CC; do not fasten off MC.

Border

Rnd 1 (rs): With rs facing and MC, ch 1, 3 sc in last st, sc evenly across to next corner, 3 sc in corner, sc in ea ch across to next corner, 3 sc in corner, sc evenly across to next corner, 3 sc in corner, sc in ea st across to next corner, change to CC in last st; join with sl st to beg sc.

Rnd 2 (ws): With CC, ch 1, turn; * sc in ea sc across to next corner, 3 sc in corner; rep from * around; join with sl st to beg sc.

Rnd 3 (rs): Ch 1, turn; * sc in ea sc across to next corner, 3 sc in corner; rep from * around, change to MC in last sc; join with sl st to beg sc.

Rnd 4 (rs): With MC, ch 1, working from left to right [reverse sc], sc in ea sc around; join with sl st to beg sc; fasten off.

Project was stitched by Joann Moss with Chenille Sensations: Mulberry #42 and Mocha #125.

Executive Stripes

Red and black make a strong statement of style.
This powerful design works well in a home office.

Materials

Chunky-weight brushed acrylic yarn, approximately: 36 oz. (1,620 yd.) burgundy, MC

Chunky-weight acrylic bouclé yarn, approximately: 36 oz. (1,110 yd.) black, CC

Size K crochet hook or size to obtain gauge

Finished Size

Approximately 50" x 65"

Gauge

In pat, 6½ sts and 8 rows = 3"

Gauge Swatch *(Multiple of 6 sts)*

With MC, ch 18. Work in pat for 15 rows.

Pattern Stitch

Long double crochet [Ldc]: Yo, insert hook from front to back in st indicated, yo and pull up long lp, (yo and pull through 2 lps) twice.

Note: Afghan is worked sideways. To change colors, work last yo of prev st with new color, dropping prev color to ws of work. Do not fasten off when changing colors.

*Color sequence: 1 row MC, * (2 rows CC, 2 rows MC) 7 times, fasten off CC, 20 rows MC; rep from * once, (2 rows CC, 2 rows MC) 7 times, 2 rows CC, 1 row MC.*

With MC, ch 138 loosely.

Row 1 (ws): Sc in 2nd ch from hook and in ea ch across: 137 sc.

Row 2 (rs): Ch 1, turn; sc in first sc and in ea sc across.

Row 3 and All Odd Rows: Ch 1, turn; sc in first sc and in ea st across.

Row 4: Ch 1, turn; sc in first sc, Ldc in 4th sc from beg 3 rows below, * sk next sc on working row, sc in next sc, Ldc in 2nd sc before prev Ldc 3 rows below [X-st made], sk next sc on working row **, sc in next 3 sc, Ldc in 6th sc from prev Ldc 3 rows below; rep from * across, ending last rep at **, sc in last sc: 23 X-sts.

Note: Be sure that X-sts interlock properly on both sides of afghan.

Row 6: Ch 1, turn; sc in first 2 sc, Ldc in 5th sc from beg 3 rows

(Continued on page 78)

below, * sk next sc on working row, sc in next sc, Ldc in 2nd sc before prev Ldc 3 rows below [X-st made], sk next sc on working row, sc in next 3 sc **, Ldc in 6th sc from prev Ldc 3 rows below; rep from * across, ending last rep at **, sc in last 3 sc: 22 X-sts.

Row 8: Ch 1, turn; sc in first 3 sc, Ldc in 6th sc from beg 3 rows below, * sk next sc on working row, sc in next sc, Ldc in 2nd sc before prev Ldc 3 rows below [X-st made], sk next sc on working row, sc in next 3 sc **, Ldc in 6th sc from prev Ldc 3 rows below; rep from * across, ending last rep at **, sc in last 2 sc: 22 X-sts.

Row 10: Ch 1, turn; sc in first 4 sc, Ldc in 7th sc from beg 3 rows below, * sk next sc on working row, sc in next sc, Ldc in 2nd sc before prev Ldc 3 rows below [X-st made], sk next sc on working row, sc in next 3 sc **, Ldc in 6th sc from prev Ldc 3 rows below; rep from * across, ending last rep at **, sc in last sc: 22 X-sts.

Row 12: Ch 1, turn; sc in first 5 sc, Ldc in 8th sc from beg 3 rows below, * sk next sc on working row, sc in next sc, Ldc in 2nd sc before prev Ldc 3 rows below [X-st made], sk next sc on working row, sc in next 3 sc **, Ldc in 6th sc from prev Ldc 3 rows below; rep from * across, ending last rep at **: 22 X-sts.

Row 14: Ch 1, turn; sc in first 6 sc, Ldc in 9th sc from beg 3 rows below, * sk next sc on working row, sc in next sc, Ldc in 2nd sc before prev Ldc 3 rows below [X-st made], sk next sc on working row **, sc in next 3 sc, Ldc in 6th sc from prev Ldc 3 rows below; rep from * across, ending last rep at **, sc in last 2 sc: 22 X-sts.

Rows 15–128: Rep rows 3–14, 9 times, then rep rows 3–8 once, changing to CC in last st of last row; do not turn after last row; fasten of MC; do not fasten off CC.

Border

Rnd 1 (rs): With rs facing and CC, ch 1, 3 sc in last st, sc evenly across to next corner, 3 sc in corner, sc in ea ch across to next corner, 3 sc in corner, sc evenly across to next corner, 3 sc in corner, sc in ea st across to next corner; join with sl st to beg sc.

Rnd 2 (ws): Ch 1, turn; * sc in ea sc across to next corner, 3 sc in corner; rep from * around; join with sl st to beg sc.

Rnd 3 (rs): Turn; sl st in same st and in ea sc around; join with sl st to beg sl st; fasten off.

Project was stitched by Madeline Speziale with Jiffy: Burgundy #142 and Homespun: Ebony #313.

Pinwheels

Stitch together four blocks with solid bands on top to make a pinwheel pattern. Just turn the blocks ninety degrees before assembling them to align the blades.

Materials

Worsted-weight wool-blend yarn, approximately:

30 oz. (1,970 yd.) brown, MC

18 oz. (1,185 yd.) red, CC

Size I crochet hook or size to obtain gauge

Yarn needle

Finished Size

Approximately 46" x 61"

Gauge

Ea Block = 7½"

Gauge Swatch (Multiple of 6 sts)

Work as for Block.

Pattern Stitch

Long double crochet [Ldc]: Yo, insert hook from front to back in st indicated, yo and pull up long lp, (yo and pull through 2 lps) twice.

Note: *To change colors, work last yo of prev st with new color, dropping prev color to ws of work. Do not fasten off when changing colors.*

Block (Make 48.)

With CC, ch 24 loosely.

Row 1 (ws): Sc in 2nd ch from hook and in ea ch across, change to MC in last st: 23 sc.

Row 2 (rs): With MC, ch 1, turn; sc in first sc and in ea sc across.

Row 3: Ch 1, turn; sc in first sc and in ea st across, change to CC in last st.

Row 4: With CC, ch 1, turn; sc in first sc, Ldc in 2nd sc from beg 3 rows below, * sk next sc on working row, sc in next sc, Ldc in 2nd sc from prev Ldc 3 rows below, sk next sc on working row **, sc in next 3 sc, Ldc in 4th sc from prev Ldc 3 rows below; rep from * across, ending last rep at **, sc in last sc: 8 Ldc.

Row 5: Ch 1, turn; sc in first sc and in ea st across, change to MC in last st.

Row 6: With MC, ch 1, turn; sc in first 4 sc, Ldc in 5th sc from beg 3 rows below, * sk next sc on working row, sc in next sc, Ldc in 2nd sc from prev Ldc 3 rows below, sk next sc on working row, sc in next 3 sc **, Ldc in 4th sc from prev Ldc 3 rows below; rep from * across, ending last rep at **, sc in last sc: 6 Ldc.

Rows 7–21: Rep rows 3–6, 3 times, then rep rows 3–5 once; fasten off CC.

Rows 22–30: Using MC throughout, rep row 6 once, then rep rows 3–6, twice; fasten off.

Assembly

Arrange 4 Blocks in pinwheel pattern, rotating 2 opposite corner blocks 90°. Whipstitch Blocks tog to form pinwheel blocks. Afghan is 3 pinwheel blocks wide and 4 pinwheel blocks long. Whipstitch blocks tog.

Border

Rnd 1 (rs): With rs facing, join MC in any corner with sl st, ch 1, * sc evenly across to next corner, 3 sc in corner; rep from * around; join with sl st to beg sc.

Rnd 2 (ws): Ch 1, turn; * sc in ea sc across to next corner, 3 sc in corner; rep from * around; join with sl st to beg sc; fasten off.

Rnd 3 (rs): With rs facing, join CC in any corner with sl st, ch 1, * 3 sc in corner, sc in ea sc across to next corner; rep from * around; join with sl st to beg sc.

Rnd 4 (rs): With rs facing and working from left to right [reverse sc], ch 1, sc in ea sc around; join with sl st to beg sc; fasten off.

Project was stitched by Marge Wild with Wool-ease: Copper #190 and Cranberry #138.

Jungle Stripes

Tigers share their stripes in chenille yarn. Bring a touch of the wild into your home with this unusual afghan.

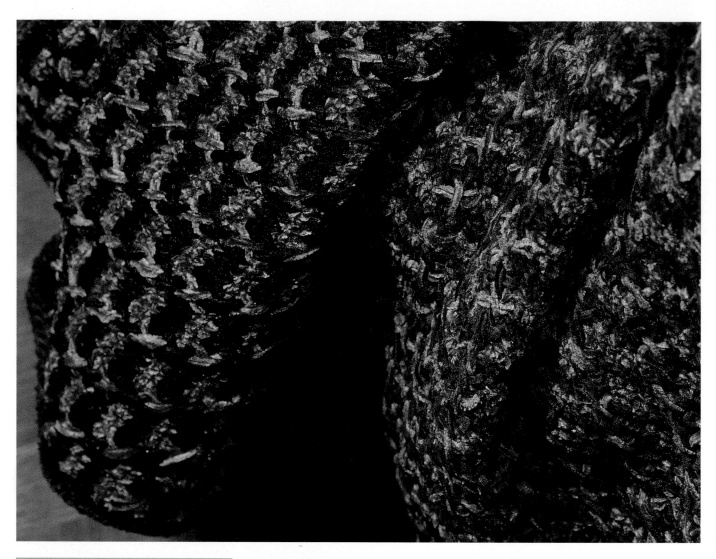

Materials
Worsted-weight chenille yarn, approximately:
27 oz. (1,655 yd.) tan, MC
17 oz. (1,045 yd.) rust, A
15½ oz. (960 yd.) black, B
Size G crochet hook or size to obtain gauge

Finished Size
Approximately 45" x 57"

Gauge
In pat, 16 sts and 18 rows = 4"

Gauge Swatch (Multiple of 6 sts)
With B, ch 18. Work in pat for 20 rows.

Pattern Stitch
Long double crochet [Ldc]: Yo, insert hook from front to back in st indicated, yo and pull up long lp, (yo and pull through 2 lps) twice.

Note: To change colors, work last yo of prev st with new color, dropping prev color to ws of work. Do not fasten off when changing colors.

Color sequence: 1 row B, (2 rows MC, 2 rows B) 7 times, (2 rows MC, 2 rows A) 49 times, fasten off A, (2 rows MC, 2 rows B) 7 times, 2 rows MC, 1 row B.

With B, ch 126 loosely.
Row 1 (ws): Sc in 2nd ch from hook and in ea ch across: 125 sc.
Row 2 (rs): Ch 1, turn; sc in first sc and in ea sc across.
Row 3 and all Odd Rows: Ch 1, turn; sc in first sc and in ea st across.
Row 4: Ch 1, turn; sc in first sc, Ldc in 4th sc from beg 3 rows below, * sk next sc on working row, sc in next sc, Ldc in 2nd sc before prev Ldc 3 rows below [X-st made], sk next sc on working row **, sc in next 3 sc, Ldc in 6th sc from prev Ldc 3 rows below; rep from * across, ending last rep at **, sc in last sc: 21 X-sts.

Note: Be sure that X-sts interlock properly on both sides of afghan.

Row 6: Ch 1, turn; sc in first 2 sc, Ldc in 5th sc from beg 3 rows below, * sk next sc on working row, sc in next sc, Ldc in 2nd sc before prev Ldc 3 rows below [X-st made], sk next sc on working row, sc in next 3 sc **, Ldc in 6th sc from prev Ldc 3 rows below; rep from * across, ending last rep at **, sc in last 3 sc: 20 X-sts.

Row 8: Ch 1, turn; sc in first 3 sc, Ldc in 6th sc from beg 3 rows below, * sk next sc on working row, sc in next sc, Ldc in 2nd sc before prev Ldc 3 rows below [X-st made], sk next sc on working row, sc in next 3 sc **, Ldc in 6th sc from prev Ldc 3 rows below; rep from * across, ending last rep at **, sc in last 2 sc: 20 X-sts.

Row 10: Ch 1, turn; sc in first 4 sc, Ldc in 7th sc from beg 3 rows below, * sk next sc on working row, sc in next sc, Ldc in 2nd sc before prev Ldc 3 rows below [X-st made], sk next sc on working row, sc in next 3 sc **, Ldc in 6th sc from prev Ldc 3 rows below; rep from * across, ending last rep at **, sc in last sc: 20 X-sts.

Row 12: Ch 1, turn; sc in first 5 sc, Ldc in 8th sc from beg 3 rows below, * sk next sc on working row, sc in next sc, Ldc in 2nd sc before prev Ldc 3 rows below

[X-st made], sk next sc on working row, sc in next 3 sc **, Ldc in 6th sc from prev Ldc 3 rows below; rep from * across, ending last rep at **: 20 X-sts.

Row 14: Ch 1, turn; sc in first 6 sc, Ldc in 9th sc from beg 3 rows below, * sk next sc on working row, sc in next sc, Ldc in 2nd sc before prev Ldc 3 rows below [X-st made], sk next sc on working row **, sc in next 3 sc, Ldc in 6th sc from prev Ldc 3 rows below; rep from * across, ending last rep at **, sc in last 2 sc: 20 X-sts.

Rows 15–256: Rep rows 3–14, 20 times, then rep rows 3 and 4 once; fasten off MC; do not fasten off B.

Left Edging

Row 1 (rs): With rs facing and B, ch 1, work 227 sc evenly across to next corner.

Rows 2–29: Rep rows 2–29 of afghan; fasten off after last row.

Right Edging

Row 1 (rs): With rs facing, join B in bottom right corner with sl st, ch 1, work 227 sc evenly across to next corner.

Rows 2–29: Rep rows 2–29 of afghan; do not fasten off.

Border

Rnd 1 (ws): With B, ch 1, turn; 3 sc in last sc, sc in ea sc across to next corner, 3 sc in corner, sc evenly across to next corner, 3 sc in corner, sc in ea sc across to next corner, 3 sc in corner, sc evenly across to next corner; join with sl st to beg sc; fasten off.

Rnd 2 (rs): With rs facing, join A in any corner with sl st, ch 1, * 3 sc in corner, sc in ea sc across to corner; rep from * around; join with sl st to beg sc.

Rnd 3 (rs): Ch 1, working from left to right [reverse sc], sc in ea sc around; join with sl st to beg sc; fasten off.

Project was stitched by Margarete Dahlke with Chenille Sensations: Brick #134, Russet #136, and Black #153.

Winter Frost

Special frosted yarn adds sparkle to this black-and-white blanket.
Separate the patterned panels with solid rows for an orderly design.

Materials
Worsted-weight wool-blend yarn, approximately:
20 oz. (1,300 yd.) white, MC
17½ oz. (1,135 yd.) black, CC
Size J crochet hook or size to obtain gauge

Finished Size
Approximately 51" x 56"

Gauge
In pat, 10 sts and 14 rows = 4"

Gauge Swatch (Multiple of 8 sts + 2)
With CC, ch 18. Work in pat for 15 rows.

Pattern Stitch
Long double crochet [Ldc]: Yo, insert hook from front to back in st indicated, yo and pull up long lp, (yo and pull through 2 lps) twice.

Note: To change colors, work last yo of prev st with new color, dropping prev color to ws of work. Do not fasten off when changing colors.

With CC, ch 122 loosely.
Row 1 (rs): Sc in 2nd ch from hook and in ea ch across: 121 sc.
Row 2 (ws): Ch 1, turn; sc in first sc and in ea st across, change to MC in last st.
Row 3: With MC, ch 1, turn; sc in first sc and in ea st across.
Row 4: Ch 1, turn; sc in first sc and in ea sc across, change to CC in last st.

Row 5: With CC, ch 1, turn; sc in first sc and in ea st across.
Rows 6–8: Rep rows 2–4 once.
Row 9: With CC, ch 1, turn; sc in first sc, Ldc in 4th sc from beg 3 rows below [slant-st made], * sk next sc on working row, sc in next 5 sc, Ldc in 2nd sc from prev Ldc 3 rows below [slant-st made], sk next sc on working row, sc in next sc **, Ldc in 6th sc from prev Ldc 3 rows below [slant-st made]; rep from * across, ending last rep at **: 30 slant-sts.
Row 10: Rep row 2.

Row 11: With MC, ch 1, turn; sc in first 2 sc, Ldc in 3rd sc from beg 3 rows below, * sk next sc on working row, sc in next sc **, Ldc in 2nd sc from prev Ldc 3 rows below; rep from * across, ending last rep at **, sc in last sc: 59 Ldc.
Row 12: Rep row 4.
Row 13: With CC, ch 1, turn; sc in first 3 sc, Ldc in 2nd sc from beg 3 rows below [slant-st made], * sk next sc on working row, sc in

(Continued on page 86)

next sc, Ldc in 6th sc from prev Ldc 3 rows below [slant-st made], sk next sc on working row **, sc in next 5 sc, Ldc in 2nd sc from prev Ldc 3 rows below [slant-st made]; rep from * across, ending last rep at **, sc in last 3 sc: 30 slant-sts.

Row 14: Rep row 2.

Row 15: Rep row 11.

Rows 16–46: Rep rows 8–15, 3 times, then rep rows 8–14 once.

Rows 47–71: Rep rows 3–11 once, then rep rows 8–11, 4 times.

Rows 72 and 73: Rep rows 8 and 9 once.

Rows 74–189: Rep rows 2–73 once, then rep rows 2–45 once.

Rows 190–194: Rep rows 2–6 once; fasten off after last row.

Right Edging

Row 1 (rs): With rs facing, join CC in bottom right corner with sl st, ch 1, sc in same st, sc evenly across to next corner.

Row 2 (ws): Ch 1, turn; sc in first sc and in ea sc across, change to MC in last st.

Row 3: With MC, ch 1, turn; sc in first sc and in ea sc across.

Row 4: Ch 1, turn; sc in first sc and in ea sc across; change to CC in last st.

Rows 5 and 6: Rep rows 2 and 3 once; fasten off after last row.

Left Edging

Row 1 (rs): With rs facing, join CC in top left corner with sl st, ch 1, sc in same st, sc evenly across to next corner.

Rows 2–6: Work as for rows 2–6 of Right Edging.

Border

With rs facing, join MC in any corner with sl st, ch 1, * sc in ea st across to next corner, 3 sc in corner, sc in ea st across to next corner; rep from * around; join with sl st to beg sc; fasten off.

Project was stitched by Margarete Dahlke with Wool-ease: White Frost #501 and Black Frost #502.

Textured Tunisian

Tunisian or afghan stitch, worked on a special hook, is fast and easy.
Post stitches add variety to the traditional stitch.

Materials

Worsted-weight wool-blend
   yarn, approximately:
39 oz. (2,565 yd.) tan, MC
36 oz. (2,365 yd.) green, CC
Size J afghan hook or size to
   obtain gauge
Size I crochet hook
Yarn needle

Finished Size

Approximately 58" x 70", without
fringe

Gauge

In pat, 10 sts and 9 rows = 3"

Gauge Swatch *(Multiple of 8 sts + 7)*

With afghan hook and CC, ch 23.
Work as for Strip B for 20 rows.

Pattern Stitch

Long stitch [L-st]: Yo, insert
hook from front to back in vertical bar indicated, yo and pull up
long lp, yo and pull through 2 lps.

*Note: See page 143 for afghan st
directions. To change colors,
work last yo of prev st with new
color; dropping prev color to ws
of work. Do not fasten off when
changing colors.*

Strip A *(Make 4.)*

With afghan hook and MC, ch 31
loosely.
Row 1: With MC, work 1 row of
afghan st, change to CC in last st:
31 sts.
Row 2: With CC, work 1 row of
afghan st.
Row 3: Work 1 row of afghan st,
change to MC in last st.

Row 4: Step 1: With MC, pick up
lp in next vertical bar, L-st in 2nd
vertical bar from beg 3 rows
below, * sk next vertical bar on
working row, pick up lp in next
vertical bar, L-st in 2nd vertical
bar from prev L-st 3 rows below,
sk next vertical bar on working
row **, pick up lps in next 5 vertical bars, L-st in 6th vertical bar
from prev L-st 3 rows below; rep
from * across, ending last rep
at **, pick up lps in last 2 vertical
bars: 8 L-sts. **Step 2:** Work as for
step 2 of afghan st.
Row 5: Rep row 1.
Row 6: Step 1: With CC, L-st in
first vertical bar from beg 3 rows
below, * sk next vertical bar on
working row, pick up lp in next
vertical bar **, L-st in 2nd vertical bar from prev L-st 3 rows
below; rep from * across, ending

last rep at **: 15 L-sts. **Step 2:** Work as for step 2 of afghan st.

Row 7: Rep row 3.

Row 8: Step 1: With MC, pick up lp in next 5 vertical bars, L-st in 6th vertical bar from beg 3 rows below, * sk next vertical bar on working row, pick up lp in next vertical bar, L-st in 2nd vertical bar from prev L-st 3 rows below, sk next vertical bar on working row, pick up lps in next 5 vertical bars **, L-st in 6th vertical bar from prev L-st 3 rows below; rep from * across, ending last rep at **, pick up lp in last vertical bar: 6 L-sts. **Step 2:** Work as for step 2 of afghan st.

Row 9: Rep row 1

Row 10: Rep row 6.

Rows 11–204: Rep rows 3–10, 24 times, then rep rows 3 and 4 once.

Row 205: With MC, sl st in ea vertical bar across; fasten off.

Strip B *(Make 3.)*

With CC and afghan hook, ch 23 loosely. Work as for Strip A, reversing colors.

Assembly

With rs facing and alternating strips, beg and ending with A, whipstitch strips tog.

Border

Rnd 1 (rs): With rs facing and crochet hook, join MC in any corner with sl st, ch 1, * 3 sc in corner, sc evenly across to next corner; rep from * around; join with sl st to beg sc; fasten off.

Rnd 2 (ws): With ws facing, join CC in top right corner with sl st, ch 1, * sc evenly across to next corner, 3 sc in corner; rep from * around; join with sl st to beg sc.

Rnd 3 (rs): Ch 1, turn; * sc in ea sc across to next corner, 3 sc in corner; rep from * around; join with sl st to beg sc; fasten off.

Rnd 4 (ws): With ws facing and MC, rep rnd 2.

Rnd 5 (rs): Turn; with rs facing and MC, sl st in corner, working across top edge, * (ch 4, sk next 2 sc, sl st in next sc) across to next corner, sl st in ea sc across side edge to next corner, sl st in corner; rep from * around; join with sl st to beg sl st; fasten off.

Fringe

For ea tassel, referring to page 143 of General Directions, cut 4 (16") lengths of CC. Working across short ends, knot 1 tassel in ea ch-4 sp.

Project was stitched by Madeline Speziale with Wool-ease: Mushroom #403 and Forest #180.

Rainbow's End

Stitch up a treasure of a throw in all the colors of the rainbow. Each vertical strip begins with the next color of the prism, creating diagonal stripes across the afghan.

Materials
Worsted-weight wool-blend
   yarn, approximately:
33 oz. (2,170 yd.) cream, MC
6 oz. (395 yd.) dark red, A
6 oz. (395 yd.) red, B
6 oz. (395 yd.) yellow, C
6 oz. (395 yd.) green, D
6 oz. (395 yd.) blue, E
6 oz. (395 yd.) purple, F
Size J crochet hook or size to
   obtain gauge
Yarn needle

Finished Size
Approximately 52" x 66"

Gauge
In pat, 9 sts and 11 rows = 3"

Gauge Swatch *(Multiple of 4 sts + 2)*
With A, ch 10. Work as for Strip 1
for 14 rows.

Pattern Stitch
Long double crochet [Ldc]: Yo,
insert hook from front to back in
st indicated, yo and pull up long
lp, (yo and pull through 2 lps)
twice.

Note: *To change colors, work
last yo of prev st with new color,
dropping prev color to ws of
work. Do not fasten off when
changing colors.*

Strip 1 *(Make 4.)*
Color sequence: *1 row A,*
* 2 rows MC, 1 row A, 1 row B,
2 rows MC, 1 row B, 1 row C,
2 rows MC, 1 row C, 1 row D,
2 rows MC, 1 row D, 1 row E,
2 rows MC, 1 row E, 1 row F,
2 rows MC, 1 row F, 1 row A;
rep from * 9 times, 2 rows MC,
1 row A.

With A, ch 10 loosely.
Row 1 (ws): Sc in 2nd ch from
hook and in ea ch across: 9 sc.
Row 2 (rs): Ch 1, turn; sc in first
sc and in ea sc across.
Row 3: Ch 1, turn; sc in first sc
and in ea st across.
Row 4: Ch 1, turn; sc in first sc,
Ldc in 3rd sc from beg 3 rows
below, * sk next sc on working
row, sc in next sc, Ldc in same sc
as prev Ldc 3 rows below [V-st
made], sk next sc on working row,
sc in next sc **, Ldc in 4th sc
from prev Ldc 3 rows below; rep
from * across, ending last rep
at **: 2 V-sts.
Rows 5–244: Rep rows 3 and 4,
120 times; fasten off after last
row.

Strip 2 *(Make 3.)*
Color sequence: *1 row B,*
* 2 rows MC, 1 row B, 1 row C,
2 rows MC, 1 row C, 1 row D,
2 rows MC, 1 row D, 1 row E,
2 rows MC, 1 row E, 1 row F,
2 rows MC, 1 row F, 1 row A,
2 rows MC, 1 row A, 1 row B;
rep from * 9 times, 2 rows MC,
1 row B.

With B, ch 10 loosely.
Work as for Strip 1.

Strip 3 *(Make 3.)*
Color sequence: *1 row C,*
* 2 rows MC, 1 row C, 1 row D,
2 rows MC, 1 row D, 1 row E,
2 rows MC, 1 row E, 1 row F,
2 rows MC, 1 row F, 1 row A,
2 rows MC, 1 row A, 1 row B,
2 rows MC, 1 row B, 1 row C;
rep from * 9 times, 2 rows MC,
1 row C.

With C, ch 10 loosely.
Work as for Strip 1.

Strip 4 *(Make 3.)*
Color sequence: *1 row D,*
* 2 rows MC, 1 row D, 1 row E,
2 rows MC, 1 row E, 1 row F,
2 rows MC, 1 row F, 1 row A,
2 rows MC, 1 row A, 1 row B,
2 rows MC, 1 row B, 1 row C,
2 rows MC, 1 row C, 1 row D;
rep from * 9 times, 2 rows MC,
1 row D.

With D, ch 10 loosely.
Work as for Strip 1.

Strip 5 *(Make 3.)*
Color sequence: *1 row E,*
* 2 rows MC, 1 row E, 1 row F,
2 rows MC, 1 row F, 1 row A,
2 rows MC, 1 row A, 1 row B,
2 rows MC, 1 row B, 1 row C,
2 rows MC, 1 row C, 1 row D,
2 rows MC, 1 row D, 1 row E;
rep from * 9 times, 2 rows MC,
1 row E.

With E, ch 10 loosely.
Work as for Strip 1.

(Continued on page 92)

Strip 6 (Make 3.)
Color sequence: *1 row F,*
* 2 rows MC, 1 row F, 1 row A,
2 rows MC, 1 row A, 1 row B,
2 rows MC, 1 row B, 1 row C,
2 rows MC, 1 row C, 1 row D,
2 rows MC, 1 row D, 1 row E,
2 rows MC, 1 row E, 1 row F;
rep from * 9 times, 2 rows MC,
1 row F.

With F, ch 10 loosely.
Work as for Strip 1.

Assembly
With rs facing, whipstitch strips
tog in foll sequence: * Strip 1,
Strip 2, Strip 3, Strip 4, Strip 5,
Strip 6; rep from * twice, Strip 1.

Border
Rnd 1 (rs): With rs facing, join
MC in any corner with sl st, ch 1,
* 3 sc in corner, sc evenly across
to next corner; rep from *
around; join with sl st to beg sc.

Rnd 2 (rs): With rs facing, sl st
in same sc and in ea sc around;
join with sl st to beg sl st; fasten
off.

*Project was stitched by Marge Wild
with Wool-ease: Fisherman #99,
Cranberry #138, Ranch Red #102,
Butterscotch #189, Hunter Green #132,
Blue Heather #107, and Plum #145.*

Candy Canes

Red and white yarns wrap around each other like the stripes on a candy cane. Finish this thick throw with evergreen borders.

Materials
Super chunky-weight wool-
blend yarn, approximately:
48 oz. (865 yd.) cream, MC
30 oz. (540 yd.) green, A
24 oz. (435 yd.) red, B
Size Q crochet hook or size
to obtain gauge

Finished Size
Approximately 54" x 71"

Gauge
In pat, 5 sts and 6 rows = 4"

Gauge Swatch (Multiple of
4 sts + 2)
With A, ch 14. Work in pat for 10
rows.

Pattern Stitch
Long double crochet [Ldc]: Yo,
insert hook from front to back in st
indicated, yo and pull up long lp,
(yo and pull through 2 lps) twice.

*Note: To change colors, work
last yo of prev st with new color,
dropping prev color to ws of
work. Do not fasten off when
changing colors.*

With A, ch 62 loosely.
Row 1 (ws): Sc in 2nd ch from
hook and in ea ch across, change
to MC in last st: 61 sc.
Row 2 (rs): With MC, ch 1, turn;
sc in first sc and in ea sc across.
Row 3: Ch 1, turn; sc in first sc
and in ea st across, change to A
in last st.

Row 4: With A, ch 1, turn; sc in
first sc, Ldc in 4th sc from beg 3
rows below [slant-st made],
* sk next sc on working row, sc in
next 3 sc **, Ldc in 4th sc from
prev Ldc 3 rows below [slant-st
made]; rep from * across, ending
last rep at **: 15 slant-sts.
Row 5: Ch 1, turn; sc in first sc
and in ea st across, change to MC
in last st.
Row 6: With MC, ch 1, turn; sc in
first 2 sc, Ldc in 3rd sc from beg
3 rows below, * sk next sc on
working row, sc in next sc **,
Ldc in 2nd sc from prev Ldc 3
rows below; rep from * across,
ending last rep at **, sc in last sc:
29 Ldc.
Rows 7–25: Rep rows 3–6, 4
times, then rep rows 3–5 once.

Row 26: With MC, ch 1, turn; sc in first 2 sc, Ldc in 3rd sc from beg 3 rows below, * sk next sc on working row **, sc in next 3 sc, Ldc in 4th sc from prev Ldc 3 rows below; rep from * across, ending last rep at **, sc in last 2 sc: 15 Ldc.

Row 27: Ch 1, turn; sc in first sc and in ea st across, change to B in last st; fasten off A.

Row 28: With B, ch 1, turn; sc in first sc, Ldc in 4th sc from beg 3 rows below [slant-st made], * sk next sc on working row, sc in next 3 sc **, Ldc in 4th sc from prev Ldc 3 rows below [slant-st made]; rep from * across, ending last rep at **: 15 slant-sts.

Row 29: Ch 1, turn; sc in first sc and in ea st across, change to MC in last st.

Rows 30–73: Rep rows 26–29, 11 times; fasten off B.

Row 74: Rep row 6.

Rows 75–100: Rep rows 3–6, 6 times, then rep rows 3 and 4 once; do not turn after last row; fasten off MC; do not fasten off A.

Border

Rnd 1 (rs): With rs facing and A, ch 1, 3 sc in last st, sc evenly across to next corner, 3 sc in corner, sc in ea ch across to next corner, 3 sc in corner, sc evenly across to next corner, 3 sc in corner, sc in ea st across to next corner, change to MC in last st; join with sl st to beg sc.

Rnd 2 (ws): With MC, ch 1, turn; * sc in ea sc across to corner, 3 sc in corner; rep from * around; join with sl st to beg sc.

Rnd 3 (rs): Ch 1, turn; * sc in ea sc across to corner, 3 sc in corner; rep from * around, change to A in last st; join with sl st to beg sc.

Rnd 4 (rs): With rs facing and A, ch 1, working from left to right [reverse sc], sc in ea sc around; join with sl st to beg sc; fasten off.

Project was stitched by Madeline Speziale with Wool-ease Thick & Quick: Fisherman #099, Pine #182, and Scarlet #113.

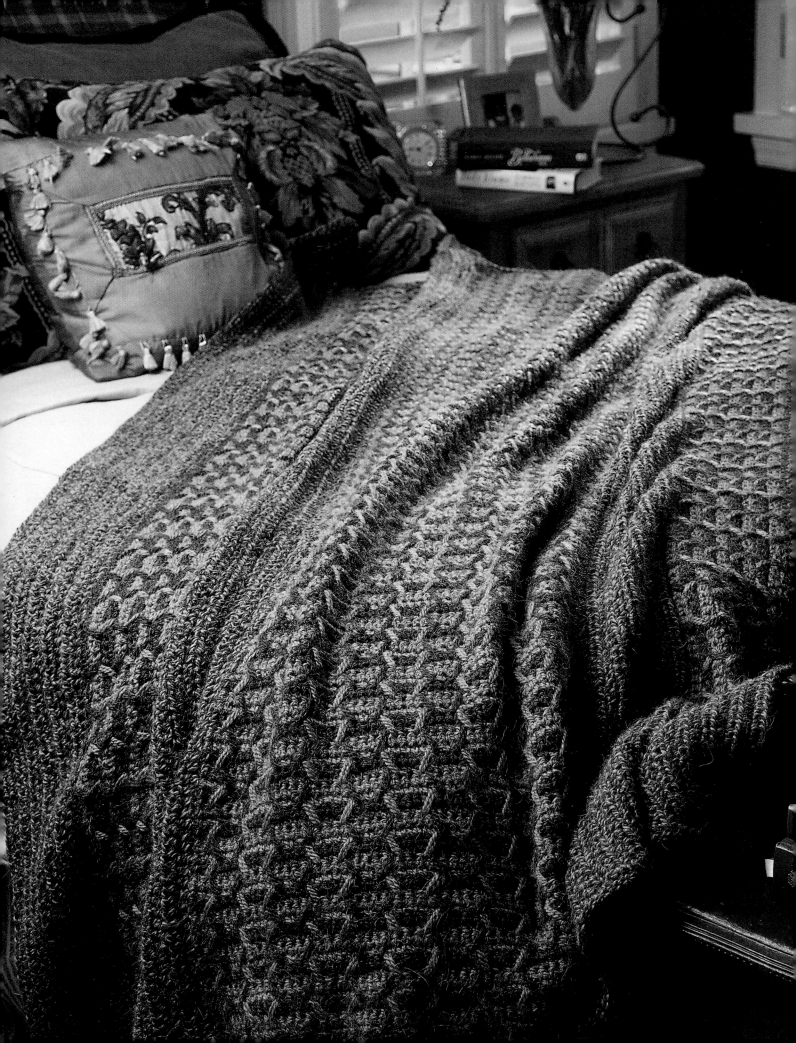

African Rhythms

This handsome blanket celebrates diverse cultures. The side panels echo the central pattern, and the two tones blend together in a variegated yarn.

Materials

Worsted-weight alpaca-wool-acrylic-blend yarn, approximately:
15¾ oz. (965 yd.) tan, MC
14 oz. (860 yd.) brown, A
17½ oz. (1,070 yd.) tan-and-brown variegated, B
Size J crochet hook or size to obtain gauge

Finished Size

Approximately 54" x 66"

Gauge

In pat, 8 sts and 10 rows = 3"

Gauge Swatch *(Multiple of 8 sts + 2)*

With A, ch 18. Work as for Center Panel for 14 rows.

Pattern Stitch

Long double crochet [Ldc]: Yo, insert hook from front to back in st indicated, yo and pull up long lp, (yo and pull through 2 lps) twice.

Note: To change colors, work last yo of prev st with new color, dropping prev color to ws of work. Do not fasten off when changing colors.

Center Panel

With A, ch 50 loosely.
Row 1 (ws): Sc in 2nd ch from hook and in ea ch across, change to MC in last st: 49 sc.
Row 2 (rs): With MC, ch 1, turn; sc in first sc and in ea sc across.
Row 3: Ch 1, turn; sc in first sc and in ea st across, change to A in last st.
Row 4: With A, ch 1, turn; sc in first sc, Ldc in 4th sc from beg 3 rows below [slant-st made], * sk next sc on working row, sc in next 5 sc, Ldc in 2nd sc from prev Ldc 3 rows below [slant-st made], sk next sc on working row, sc in next sc **, Ldc in 6th sc from prev Ldc 3 rows below [slant-st made]; rep from * across, ending last rep at **: 12 slant-sts.
Row 5: Ch 1, turn; sc in first sc and in ea st across, change to MC in last st.
Row 6: With MC, ch 1, turn; sc in first 3 sc, Ldc in 2nd sc from beg 3 rows below [slant-st made], * sk next sc on working row, sc in next sc, Ldc in 6th sc from prev Ldc 3 rows below [slant-st made], sk next sc on working row **, sc in next 5 sc, Ldc in 2nd sc from prev Ldc 3 rows below [slant-st made]; rep from * across, ending last rep at **, sc in last 3 sc: 12 slant sts.
Rows 7–220: Rep rows 3–6, 53 times, then rep rows 3 and 4 once; fasten off.

Left Side Panel

Row 1 (rs): With rs facing, join B in top left corner with sl st, ch 1, work 177 sc evenly across to next corner: 177 sc.
Rows 2–13: Ch 2, turn; hdc in first st and in ea st across, change to A in last st of last row: 177 hdc.
Row 14: With A, ch 1, turn; sc in first hdc and in ea hdc across, change to MC in last st.
Row 15: With MC, ch 1, turn; sc in first sc and in ea sc across.
Rows 16–33: Rep rows 3–6 of Center Panel, 4 times, then rep rows 3 and 4 of Center Panel once, change to B in last st of last row.
Rows 34–45: Rep row 2, 12 times; fasten off.

Right Side Panel

Row 1 (rs): With rs facing, join B in bottom right corner with sl st, ch 1, work 177 sc evenly across to next corner: 177 sc.
Rows 2–45: Work as for rows 2–45 of Right Side Panel; do not fasten off B.

Border

Rnd 1 (ws): With B, ch 1, turn; sc in last hdc and in ea hdc across to next corner, 3 sc in corner, sc evenly across to next corner, 3 sc in corner, sc in ea hdc across to next corner, 3 sc in corner, sc evenly across to next corner, 2 sc in corner; join with sl st to beg sc.
Rnd 2 (rs): Turn; sl st in same sc and in ea sc around; join with sl st to beg sl st; fasten off.

Project was stitched by Margarete Dahlke with Al-Pa-Ka: Camel #124, Mink Brown #127, and Camel Tweed #224.

Tricolored Vest

Make this striking vest for a man or a woman; we list all sizes in the directions. Stitch the center panels for the front and the back first. Then work the side panels up and over the shoulders.

Materials

Worsted-weight alpaca-wool-acrylic-blend yarn, approximately:
7 {7, 8¾, 8¾, 10½, 10½} oz. (430 {430, 535, 535, 645, 645} yd.) black-and-gray variegated, MC
3½ {3½, 3½, 3½, 5¼, 5¼} oz. (215 {215, 215, 215, 325, 325} yd.) black, A
3½ {3½, 3½, 3½, 5¼, 5¼} oz. (215 {215, 215, 215, 325, 325} yd.) dark gray, B
3½ {3½, 3½, 3½, 5¼, 5¼} oz. (215 {215, 215, 215, 325, 325} yd.) light gray, C
Sizes I and J crochet hooks or sizes to obtain gauge
Yarn needle

Note: Directions are written for women's size small, with women's sizes medium and large and men's sizes small, medium, and large in braces { }. Circle all numbers pertaining to desired size before beginning.

Finished Size

Chest: 40" {44", 48", 52", 55", 59"}
Length: 25" {25", 26", 26", 27", 27"}

Gauge

In pat with larger hook, 8 sts and 10 rows = 3"
8 hdc and 6 rows = 3"

Gauge Swatch *(Multiple of 4 sts + 2)*

With A, ch 14. Work as for Back Center Panel for 15 rows.

Pattern Stitches

Long double crochet [Ldc]: Yo, insert hook from front to back in st indicated, yo and pull up long lp, (yo and pull through 2 lps) twice.

Decrease [dec]: [Worked over 2 sts] Yo, insert hook in st indicated, yo and pull up lp, yo, insert hook in next st, yo and pull up lp, yo and pull through all 5 lps on hook.

Note: To change colors, work last yo of prev st with new color, dropping prev color to ws of work. Do not fasten off when changing colors.

Back Center Panel

With larger hook and A, ch 22 loosely.

Row 1 (ws): Sc in 2nd ch from hook and in ea ch across, change to B in last st: 21 sc.

Row 2 (rs): With B, ch 1, turn; sc in first sc and in ea sc across, change to C in last st.

Row 3: With C, ch 1, turn; sc in first sc and in ea st across, change to A in last st.

Row 4: With A, ch 1, turn; sc in first sc, Ldc in 3rd sc from beg 3 rows below, * sk next sc on working row, sc in next sc, Ldc in same sc as prev Ldc [V-st made], sk next sc on working row, sc in next sc **, Ldc in 4th sc from prev Ldc; rep from * across, ending last rep at **, change to B in last st: 5 V-sts.

Row 5: With B, ch 1, turn; sc in first sc and in ea st across, change to C in last st.

Row 6: With C, ch 1, turn; sc in first 3 sc, Ldc in 5th sc from beg 3 rows below, * sk next sc on working row, sc in next sc, Ldc in same sc as prev Ldc 3 rows below [V-st made], sk next sc on working row, sc in next sc **, Ldc in 4th sc from prev Ldc 3 rows below; rep from * across, ending last rep at **, sc in last 2 sc, change to A in last st: 4 V-sts.

Row 7: With A, ch 1, turn; sc in first sc and in ea st across, change to B in last st.

Row 8: With B, ch 1, turn; work as for row 4, change to C in last st: 5 V-sts.

Row 9: With C, ch 1, turn; sc in first sc and in ea st across, change to A in last st.

Row 10: With A, ch 1, turn; work as for row 6, change to B in last st: 4 V-sts.

Row 11: Rep row 5.

Row 12: With C, ch 1, turn; work as for row 4, change to A in last st: 5 V-sts.

Row 13: Rep row 7.

Row 14: With B, ch 1, turn; work as for row 6, change to C in last st: 4 V-sts.

Row 15: Rep row 9.

Rows 16–72 {16–72, 16–74, 16–74, 16–78, 16–78}: Rep rows 4–15, 4 {4, 4, 4, 5, 5} times, then rep rows 4–12 {4–12, 4–14, 4–14, 4–6, 4–6} once; fasten off.

(Continued on page 100)

Front Center Panel

Work as for Back Center Panel for 64 rows.

Left Side Panel

Row 1 (rs): With rs facing and larger hook, join MC in bottom right corner of Front Center Panel with sl st, ch 1, work 51 {51, 54, 54, 57, 57} sc evenly across side edge to next corner, ch 8 loosely [neck opening], sc in top left corner of Back Center Panel, work 56 {56, 59, 59, 62, 62} sc evenly across side edge to next corner: 116 {116, 122, 122, 128, 128} sts.

Row 2 (ws): Ch 1, turn; hdc in next 58 {58, 61, 61, 64, 64} sts, place marker [center], hdc in next 58 {58, 61, 61, 64, 64} sts: 116 {116, 122, 122, 128, 128} hdc.

Row 3 [women's size small only]: Ch 1, turn; hdc in first 56 hdc, (dec in next 2 hdc) twice, hdc in last 56 hdc: 114 hdc.

Row 3 [all other sizes]: Ch 1, turn; hdc in first hdc and in each hdc across: {116, 122, 122, 128, 128} hdc.

Row 4 [women's size small only]: Ch 1, turn; hdc in first hdc and in each hdc across: 114 hdc.

Row 4 [all other sizes]: Ch 1, turn; hdc in first {56, 59, 59, 62, 62} hdc, (dec in next 2 hdc) twice, hdc in last {56, 59, 59, 62, 62} hdc: {114, 120, 120, 126, 126} hdc.

Row 5 [women's size small only]: Ch 1, turn; hdc in first 55 hdc, (dec in next 2 hdc) twice, hdc in last 55 hdc: 112 hdc.

Row 5 [all other sizes]: Ch 1, turn; hdc in first hdc and in each hdc across: {114, 120, 120, 126, 126} hdc.

Row 6 [women's size small; men's sizes small, medium, and large]: Ch 1, turn; hdc in first hdc and in each hdc across: 112 {120, 126, 126} hdc.

Row 6 [women's sizes medium and large]: Ch 1, turn; hdc in

first 55 {58} hdc, (dec in next 2 hdc) twice, hdc in last 55 {58} hdc: 112 {118} hdc.

Row 7 [women's size small; men's sizes small, medium, and large]: Ch 1, turn; hdc in first 54 {58, 61, 61} hdc, (dec in next 2 hdc) twice, hdc in last 54 {58, 61, 61} hdc: 110 {118, 124, 124} hdc.

Row 7 [women's sizes medium and large]: Ch 1, turn; hdc in first hdc and in ea hdc across: 112 {118} hdc.

Row 8 [women's size small; men's sizes small, medium, and large]: Ch 1, turn; hdc in first hdc and in ea hdc across: 110 {118, 124, 124} hdc.

Row 8 [women's sizes medium and large]: Ch 1, turn; hdc in first 54 {57} hdc, (dec in next 2 hdc) twice, hdc in last 54 {57} hdc: 110 {116} hdc.

Row 9 [all remaining sizes]: Ch 1, turn; hdc in first hdc and in ea hdc across: {110, 116, 118, 124, 124} hdc.

Note: Last row for women's size medium; do not fasten off; refer to First Armhole Shaping.

Row 10 [women's size large]: Ch 1, turn; hdc in first hdc and in ea hdc across: {116} hdc.

Row 10 [men's sizes small, medium, and large]: Ch 1, turn; hdc in first {57, 60, 60} hdc, (dec in next 2 hdc) twice, hdc in last {57, 60, 60} hdc: {116, 122, 122} hdc.

Row 11 [all remaining sizes]: Ch 1, turn; hdc in first hdc and in ea hdc across: {116, 116, 122, 122} hdc.

Note: Last row for women's size large; do not fasten off; refer to First Armhole Shaping.

Rows 12 and 13 [all remaining sizes]: Ch 1, turn; hdc in first hdc and in ea hdc across: {116, 122, 122 hdc}.

Note: Last row for men's sizes small and medium; do not fasten off; refer to First Armhole Shaping.

Row 14 [men's size large]: Ch 1, turn; hdc in first hdc and in ea hdc across: {122} hdc.

First Armhole Shaping
Row 1: Ch 1, turn; hdc in first 33 {33, 33, 33, 34, 34} hdc.
Row 2 [women's size small

and men's size large]: Ch 1, turn; dec in first 2 hdc, hdc in next hdc and in ea hdc across: 32 {33} hdc.

Row 2 [women's sizes medium and large; men's sizes small and medium]: Ch 1, turn; hdc in first hdc and in ea hdc across to last 2 hdc, dec in last 2 hdc: {32, 32, 32, 33} hdc.

Row 3 [women's size small and men's size large]: Ch 1, turn; hdc in first hdc and in ea hdc across to last 2 sts, dec in last 2 sts: 31 {32} hdc.

Row 3 [women's sizes medium and large; men's sizes small and medium]: Ch 1, turn; dec in first 2 sts, hdc in next hdc and in ea hdc across: {31, 31, 31, 32} hdc.

Row 4 [all sizes]: Ch 1, turn; hdc in first st and in ea st across: 31 {31, 31, 31, 32, 32} hdc.

Note: Last row for women's size small; fasten off; refer to Second Armhole Shaping.

Row 5 [all remaining sizes]: Ch 1, turn; hdc in first st and in ea st across: {31, 31, 31, 32, 32} hdc.

Note: Last row for women's sizes medium and large and for men's sizes small and medium; fasten off; refer to Second Armhole Shaping.

Row 6 [men's size large]: Ch 1, turn; hdc in first st and in ea st across; fasten off: {32} hdc.

Second Armhole Shaping
Row 1 (ws): With ws facing and larger hook, join MC in top left corner with sl st [last full row worked]; ch 2, hdc in same st and in next 32 {32, 32, 32, 33, 33} hdc: 33 {33, 33, 33, 34, 34} hdc.
Row 2: Ch 1, turn; dec in first 2 hdc, hdc in next hdc and in ea

hdc across: 32 {32, 32, 32, 33, 33} hdc.
Row 3: Ch 1 turn; hdc in first hdc and in ea hdc across to last 2 sts, dec in last 2 sts: 31 {31, 31, 31, 32, 32} hdc.
Rows 4–6: Work as for rows 4–6 of First Armhole Shaping.

Right Side Panel
Row 1 (rs): With rs facing and larger hook, join MC in bottom right corner of Back Center Panel with sl st, ch 1, work 57 {57, 60, 60, 63, 63} sc evenly across side edge to next corner, ch 8 loosely [neck opening], sc in top left corner of Front Center Panel, work 51 {51, 54, 54, 57, 57} sc evenly across side edge to next corner: 116 {116, 122, 122, 128, 128} sc.
Rows 2–14: Work as for rows 2–14 of Left Side Panel.

First Armhole Shaping
Work as for Second Armhole Shaping for Left Side Panel.

Second Armhole Shaping
Work as for First Armhole Shaping for Left Side Panel.

Assembly
With rs facing, whipstitch side seams tog, leaving Armholes unstitched.

Ribbing
Color sequence: (1 row A, 1 row B, 1 row C) 46 {48, 54, 60, 64, 70} times.

With A and smaller hook, ch 12 loosely.
Row 1 (rs): Sc in 2nd ch from hook and in ea ch across: 11 sc.
Rows 2–138 {2–144, 2–162, 2–180, 2–192, 2–210}: Ch 1, turn; sc in first sc, sc in bk lps only of next 9 sc, sc in both lps of last sc; fasten off after last row. With rs facing, whipstitch first

and last rows of Ribbing tog. With rs tog, whipstitch Ribbing to bottom of Vest.

Right Armhole Trim
Rnd 1 (rs): With rs facing and larger hook, join A at bottom of Right Armhole with sl st, ch 1, sc evenly around; join with sl st to beg sc.

Note: Change to smaller hook.

Rnd 2 (rs): With smaller hook, ch 1, working from left to right [reverse sc], sc in ea sc around; join with sl st to beg sc; fasten off.

Left Armhole Trim
Rnd 1 (rs): With rs facing and larger hook, join A at bottom of Left Armhole with sl st, ch 1, sc evenly around; join with sl st to beg sc.

Note: Change to smaller hook.

Rnd 2 (rs): Work as for rnd 2 of Right Armhole Trim.

Neck Trim
Rnd 1 (rs): With rs facing and larger hook, join B at side of Neck with sl st, ch 1, sc evenly around; join with sl st to beg sc.

Note: Change to smaller hook.

Rnd 2 (rs): With smaller hook, ch 1, working from left to right [reverse sc], sc in first sc and in ea sc around; join with sl st to beg sc; fasten off.

Project was stitched by Margarete Dahlke with Al-Pa-Ka: Oxford Tweed #252, Black #153, Oxford Grey #152, and Silver Grey #149.

Blue Waves

Achieve the look of a ripple afghan without all the increases and the decreases. Work each row straight across but add slanted post stitches to create visual peaks and valleys.

Materials

Chunky-weight acrylic bouclé yarn, approximately:
36 oz. (1,110 yd.) dark blue, MC
24 oz. (740 yd.) light blue, A
12 oz. (370 yd.) tan, B
Size K crochet hook or size to obtain gauge

Finished Size

Approximately 45" x 53"

Gauge

In pat, 7 sts and 8 rows = 3"

Gauge Swatch *(Multiple of 10 sts + 6)*

With MC, ch 16. Work in pat for 14 rows.

Pattern Stitches

Long double crochet [Ldc]: Yo, insert hook from front to back in st indicated, yo and pull up long lp, (yo and pull through 2 lps) twice.

Front Post double crochet [FPdc]: Yo, insert hook from front to back around post of st indicated, yo and pull up lp, (yo and pull through 2 lps) twice.

Note: *To change colors, work last yo of prev st with new color, dropping prev color to ws of work. Do not fasten off when changing colors.*

Color sequence: *1 row MC, * (2 rows A, 2 rows MC) 5 times, (2 rows B, 2 rows MC) twice, 2 rows A, 2 rows MC, (2 rows B, 2 rows MC) twice, fasten off B; rep from * twice, (2 rows A, 2 rows MC) 4 times, 2 rows A, 1 row MC.*

With MC, ch 106 loosely.

Row 1 (ws): Sc in 2nd ch from hook and in ea ch across: 105 sc.

Row 2 (rs): Ch 1, turn; sc in first sc and in ea sc across.

Row 3 and all Odd Rows: Ch 1, turn; sc in first sc and in ea st across.

Row 4: Ch 1, turn; sc in first 2 sc, Ldc in 3rd sc from beg 3 rows below, * sk next sc on working row, sc in next sc **, Ldc in 3rd sc from prev Ldc 3 rows below [slant-st made], sk next sc on working row, sc in next sc, Ldc in

(Continued on page 104)

2nd sc from prev Ldc 3 rows below, sk next sc on working row, sc in next sc, Ldc in same sc as prev Ldc 3 rows below [V-st made], sk next sc on working row, sc in next sc, Ldc in 2nd sc from prev Ldc 3 rows below [slant-st made], sk next sc on working row, sc in next sc, Ldc in 3rd sc from prev Ldc 3 rows below; rep from * across, ending last rep at **, sc in last sc: 10 Ldc, 18 slant-sts and 9 V-sts.

Row 6: Ch 1, turn; sc in first 2 sc, FPdc around first Ldc 3 rows below, * sk next sc on working row, sc in next sc **, Ldc in 3rd sc from prev Ldc 3 rows below [slant-st made], sk next sc on working row, sc in next sc, Ldc in 2nd sc from prev Ldc 3 rows below, sk next sc on working row, sc in next sc, Ldc in same sc as prev Ldc 3 rows below [V-st made], sk next sc on working row, sc in next sc, Ldc in 2nd sc from prev Ldc 3 rows below [slant-st made], sk next sc on working row, sc in next sc, FPdc around next

Ldc 3 rows below; rep from * across, ending last rep at **, sc in last sc: 10 FPdc, 18 slant-sts and 9 V-sts.

Row 8: Ch 1, turn; sc in first 2 sc, FPdc around first FPdc 3 rows below, * sk next sc on working row, sc in next sc **, Ldc in 3rd sc from prev FPdc 3 rows below [slant-st made], sk next sc on working row, sc in next sc, Ldc in 2nd sc from prev Ldc 3 rows below, sk next sc on working row, sc in next sc, Ldc in same sc as prev Ldc 3 rows below [V-st made], sk next sc on working row, sc in next sc, Ldc in 2nd sc from prev Ldc 3 rows below [slant-st made], sk next sc on working row, sc in next sc, FPdc around next FPdc 3 rows below; rep from * across, ending last rep at **, sc in last sc: 10 FPdc, 18 slant-sts and 9 V-sts.

Rows 9–140: Rep rows 7 and 8, 66 times; do not turn after last row; fasten off A and B; do not fasten off MC.

Border

Rnd 1 (rs): With rs facing and MC, ch 1, 3sc in last st, sc evenly across to next corner, 3 sc in corner, sc in ea ch across to next corner, 3 sc in corner, sc evenly across to next corner, 3 sc in corner, sc in ea st across to next corner; join with sl st to beg sc; fasten off.

Rnd 2 (ws): With ws facing, join B in any corner with sl st, ch 1, * 3 sc in corner, sc in ea sc across to next corner; rep from * around; join with sl st to beg sc; fasten off.

Rnd 3 (rs): With rs facing, join MC in any corner with sl st, ch 1, * 3 sc in corner, sc in ea sc across to next corner; rep from * around; join with sl st to beg sc; fasten off.

Project was stitched by Peggy Stiver with Homespun: Colonial #302, Williamsburg #321, and Rococo #311.

Scottish Plaid

This attractive blanket focuses on a single square from a plaid design.
Choose your tartan colors and create a family heirloom.

Materials

Worsted-weight cotton yarn,
approximately:
40 oz. (1,890 yd.) black, MC
15 oz. (710 yd.) sage, A
15 oz. (710 yd.) blue, B
Size I crochet hook or size to
obtain gauge
Yarn needle

Finished Size

Approximately 52" x 62"

Gauge

In pat, 11 sts and 14 rows = 4"

Gauge Swatch *(Multiple of 12 sts + 8)*

With B, ch 20. Work as for Panel
B for 19 rows.

Pattern Stitch

Long double crochet [Ldc]: Yo,
insert hook from front to back in
st indicated, yo and pull up long
lp, (yo and pull through 2 lps)
twice.

Note: *To change colors, work
last yo of prev st with new color,
dropping prev color to ws of
work. Do not fasten off when
changing colors.*

Center Panel

Color sequence: *1 row B,
(2 rows MC, 2 rows B) 5 times,
2 rows MC, 1 row B, fasten off B,
(2 rows MC, 2 rows A) 5 times,
2 rows MC, 1 row A, fasten off A,
(2 rows MC, 2 rows B) 30 times,
2 rows MC, 1 row B, fasten off B,
(2 rows MC, 2 rows A) 5 times,*
*2 rows MC, 1 row A, fasten off A,
(2 rows MC, 2 rows B) 5 times,
2 rows MC, 1 row B.*

With B, ch 68 loosely.

Row 1 (ws): Sc in 2nd ch from
hook and in ea ch across: 67 sc.
Row 2 (rs): Ch 1, turn; sc in first
sc and in ea sc across.
Row 3 and all Odd Rows: Ch 1,
turn; sc in first sc and in ea st
across.
Row 4: Ch 1, turn; sc in first 2 sc,
Ldc in 4th sc from beg 3 rows
below, * sk next sc on working
row, sc in next sc, Ldc in same sc
as prev Ldc 3 rows below [V-st
made], sk next sc on working row,
sc in next sc **, Ldc in 3rd sc
from prev Ldc 3 rows below,
sk next sc on working row, sc in
next sc, Ldc in 4th sc from prev

Ldc 3 rows below, sk next sc on working row, sc in next sc, Ldc in 2nd sc before prev Ldc 3 rows below [X-st made], sk next sc on working row, sc in next sc, Ldc in 2nd sc from prev Ldc 3 rows below, sk next sc on working row, sc in next sc, Ldc in 3rd sc from prev Ldc 3 rows below; rep from * across, ending last rep at **, sc in last sc: 6 V-sts, 10 Ldc, and 5 X-sts.

Row 6: Ch 1, turn; sc in first sc, Ldc in 2nd sc from beg 3 rows below, * sk next sc on working row, sc in next 3 sc, Ldc in 4th sc from prev Ldc 3 rows below, sk next sc on working row, sc in next sc **, Ldc in 2nd sc from prev Ldc 3 rows below; rep from * across, ending last rep at **: 22 Ldc.

Rows 7–216: Rep rows 3–6, 52 times, then rep rows 3 and 4 once; fasten off after last row.

Panel A (Make 2.)

Color sequence: 1 row MC, (2 rows A, 2 rows MC) 5 times, 2 rows A, fasten off A, 1 row MC, (2 rows B, 2 rows MC) 5 times, 2 rows B, fastem off B, 1 row MC, (2 rows A, 2 rows MC) 30 times, 2 rows A, fasten off A, 1 row MC, (2 rows B, 2 rows MC) 5 times, 2 rows B, fasten off B, 1 row MC, (2 rows A, 2 rows MC) 5 times, 2 rows A, 1 row MC.

With MC, ch 20 loosely.

Row 1 (rs): Sc in 2nd ch from hook and in ea ch across: 19 sc.

Row 2 (ws): Ch 1, turn; sc in first sc and in ea sc across.

Row 3 and all Odd Rows: Ch 1, turn; sc in first sc and in ea st across.

Row 4: Ch 1, turn; sc in first 2 sc, Ldc in 5th sc from beg 3 rows below, * sk next sc on working row, sc in next sc, Ldc in 2nd sc before prev Ldc 3 rows below [X-st made], sk next sc on working row, sc in next sc **, Ldc in 2nd sc from prev Ldc 3 rows below, sk next sc on working row, sc in next sc, Ldc in 3rd sc from prev Ldc 3 rows below, sk next sc on working row, sc in next sc, Ldc in same sc as prev Ldc 3 rows below [V-st made], sk next sc on working row, sc in next sc, Ldc in 3rd sc from prev Ldc 3 rows below, sk next sc on working row, sc in next sc, Ldc in 4th sc from prev Ldc 3 rows below; rep from * to ** once, sc in last sc: 2 X-sts, 2 Ldc, and 1 V-st.

Row 6: Ch 1, turn; sc in first sc, Ldc in 2nd sc from beg 3 rows below, * sk next sc on working row, sc in next 3 sc, Ldc in 4th sc from prev Ldc 3 rows below, sk next sc on working row, sc in next sc **, Ldc in 2nd sc from prev Ldc 3 rows below; rep from * across, ending last rep at **: 6 Ldc.

Rows 7–216: Rep rows 3–6, 52 times, then rep rows 3 and 4 once; fasten off after last row.

Panel B (Make 2.)
With B, ch 20 loosely.
Work as for Center Panel; fasten off.

Assembly
With rs facing, arrange panels in foll sequence: Panel B, Panel A, Center Panel, Panel A, Panel B. Whipstitch Panels tog.

Border
Rnd 1 (rs): With rs facing, join A in any corner with sl st, ch 1, * 3 sc in corner, sc evenly across to next corner; rep from * around; join with sl st to beg sc.

Rnd 2 (ws): Turn; with ws facing, sl st in same st and in ea st around; join with sl st to beg sl st; fasten off.

Project was stitched by Madeline Speziale with Kitchen Cotton: Black #153, Sage #181, and Morning Glory Blue #108.

Zebra Zigzags

Give your home an exotic look with a daring afghan bordered with zany stripes.

Materials
Chunky-weight brushed acrylic yarn, approximately:
36 oz. (1,620 yd.) gray, MC
18 oz. (810 yd.) black, CC
Size K crochet hook or size to obtain gauge

Finished Size
Approximately 52" x 59"

Gauge
In pat, 10 sts and 11 rows = 4"

Gauge Swatch (*Multiple of 8 sts + 6*)
With CC, ch 22. Work in pat for 20 rows.

Pattern Stitch
Long double crochet [Ldc]:
Yo, insert hook from front to back in st indicated, yo and pull up long lp, (yo and pull through 2 lps) twice.

Note: To change colors, work last yo of prev st with new color, dropping prev color to ws of work. Do not fasten off when changing colors.

Color sequence: 1 row CC, (2 rows MC, 2 rows CC) 9 times, fasten off CC, 82 rows MC, (2 rows CC, 2 rows MC) 9 times, 1 row CC.

With CC, ch 126 loosely.
Row 1 (ws): Sc in 2nd ch from hook and in ea ch across: 125 sc.
Row 2 (rs): Ch 1, turn; sc in first sc and in ea sc across.

Row 3 and all Odd Rows: Ch 1, turn; sc in first sc and in ea st across.

Row 4: Ch 1, turn; sc in first sc, Ldc in 2nd sc from beg 3 rows below, * sk next sc on working row, sc in next sc, Ldc in 2nd sc from prev Ldc 3 rows below, sk next sc on working row **, sc in next 5 sc, Ldc in 6th sc from prev Ldc 3 rows below; rep from * across, ending last rep at **, sc in last sc: 32 Ldc.

Row 6: Ch 1, turn; sc in first 2 sc, Ldc in 3rd sc from beg 3 rows below, * sk next sc on working row, sc in next sc **, Ldc in 2nd sc from prev Ldc 3 rows below, sk next sc on working row, sc in next 5 sc, Ldc in 6th sc from prev Ldc 3 rows below; rep from * across, ending last rep at **, sc in last sc: 31 Ldc.

Row 8: Ch 1, turn; sc in first 3 sc, Ldc in 4th sc from beg 3 rows below, * sk next sc on working row, sc in next sc **, Ldc in 2nd sc from prev Ldc 3 rows below, sk next sc on working row, sc in next 5 sc, Ldc in 6th sc from prev Ldc 3 rows below; rep from * across, ending last rep at **: 31 Ldc.

Row 10: Ch 1, turn; sc in first 4 sc, Ldc in 5th sc from beg 3 rows below, * sk next sc on working row, sc in next sc, Ldc in 2nd sc from prev Ldc 3 rows below, sk next sc on working row, sc in next 5 sc **, Ldc in 6th sc from prev Ldc 3 rows below; rep from * across, ending last rep at **, sc in last sc: 30 Ldc.

Row 12: Ch 1, turn; sc in first 5 sc, Ldc in 6th sc from beg 3 rows below, * sk next sc on working row, sc in next sc, Ldc in 2nd sc from prev Ldc 3 rows below, sk next sc on working row, sc in next 5 sc **, Ldc in 6th sc from prev Ldc 3 rows below; rep from * across, ending last rep at **: 30 Ldc.

Row 14: Ch 1, turn; sc in first 6 sc, Ldc in 7th sc from beg 3 rows below, * sk next sc on working row, sc in next sc, Ldc in 2nd sc from prev Ldc 3 rows below, sk next sc on working row **, sc in next 5 sc, Ldc in 6th sc from prev Ldc 3 rows below; rep from * across, ending last rep at **, sc in last 4 sc: 30 Ldc.

Row 16: Ch 1, turn; sc in first sc, Ldc in 2nd sc from beg 3 rows below, * sk next sc on working row **, sc in next 5 sc, Ldc in 6th sc from prev Ldc 3 rows below, sk next sc on working row, sc in next sc, Ldc in 2nd sc from prev Ldc 3 rows below; rep from * across, ending last rep at **, sc in last 3 sc: 31 Ldc.

Row 18: Ch 1, turn; sc in first 2 sc, Ldc in 3rd sc from beg 3 rows below, * sk next sc on working row **, sc in next 5 sc, Ldc in 6th sc from prev Ldc 3 rows below, sk next sc on working row, sc in next sc, Ldc in 2nd sc from prev Ldc 3 rows below; rep from * across, ending last rep at **, sc in last 2 sc: 31 Ldc.

Rows 19–156: Rep rows 3–18, 8 times, then rep rows 3–12 once; fasten off after last row.

(Continued on page 110)

Border

Rnd 1 (rs): With rs facing, join MC in top right corner with sl st, ch 1, 3 sc in same st, sc in ea st across to next corner, 3 sc in corner, sc evenly across to next corner, 3 sc in corner, sc in ea ch across to next corner, 3 sc in corner, sc evenly across to next corner, change to CC in last st; join with sl st to beg sc; fasten off MC.

Rnd 2 (ws): With CC, ch 1, turn; * sc in ea st across to corner, 3 sc in corner; rep from * around; join with sl st to beg sc.

Rnd 3 (rs): Ch 1, turn; * sc in ea st across to corner, 3 sc in corner; rep from * around; join with sl st to beg sc; fasten off.

Project was stitched by Madeline Speziale with Jiffy: Silver #149 and Black #153.

Jazzy Jacket

Get two looks from one fully reversible garment. This cozy cardigan has turned-up cuffs and a simple lapel to show off both patterns at once.

Materials

Chunky-weight brushed acrylic yarn, approximately: 24 {24, 27, 27, 30, 30, 33} oz. (1,080 {1,080; 1,215; 1,215; 1,350; 1,350; 1,485} yd.) fuchsia, MC

Chunky-weight acrylic bouclé yarn, approximately: 30 {30, 36, 36, 42, 42, 48} oz. (925 {925; 1,110; 1,110; 1,295; 1,295; 1,480} yd.) blue-and-turquoise variegated, CC

Size K crochet hook or size to obtain gauge

Yarn needle

Note: Directions are written for women's size petite, with sizes small, medium, large, extra-large, extra-extra-large, and extra-extra-extra-large in braces { }. Circle all numbers pertaining to desired size before beginning.

Finished Size

Chest: 40" {43½", 47", 50½", 54", 57½", 61"}

Length: 25⅓" {26⅔", 26⅔", 26⅔", 28", 28", 28"}

Gauge

In pat, 7 sts and 9 rows = 3"

Gauge Swatch *(Multiple of 4 sts)*

With MC, ch 16. Work as for Back for 16 rows.

Pattern Stitches

Front Post double crochet cluster [FPdccl]: Insert hook in next st on working row, yo and pull up lp, yo, insert hook from front to back around post of next st indicated, yo and pull up lp, (yo and pull through 2 lps) 3 times.

Long double crochet [Ldc]: Yo, insert hook from front to back in st indicated, yo and pull up long lp, (yo and pull through 2 lps) twice.

Decrease [dec]: [Worked over 2 sts] Insert hook in st indicated, yo and pull up lp, insert hook in next st, yo and pull up lp, yo and pull through all 3 lps on hook.

Note: To change colors, work last yo of prev st with new color, dropping prev color to ws of work. Do not fasten off when changing colors.

Back

With MC, ch 48 {52, 56, 60, 64, 68, 72} loosely.

Row 1 (ws): Sc in 2nd ch from hook and in ea ch across, change to CC in last st: 47 {51, 55, 59, 63, 67, 71} sc.

Row 2 (rs): With CC, ch 1, turn; sc in first sc and in ea sc across.

Row 3: Ch 1, turn; sc in first sc and in ea st across, change to MC in last st.

Row 4: With MC, ch 1, turn; sc in first 4 sc, FPdccl around 3rd sc from beg 3 rows below, * sc in

next 3 sc, FPdccl around 4th sc from prev FPdccl 3 rows below; rep from * across, sc in last 2 sc: 11 {12, 13, 14, 15, 16, 17} FPdccl.
Row 5: Ch 1, turn; sc in first sc and in ea st across, change to CC in last st.
Row 6: With CC, ch 1, turn; sc in first sc, Ldc in 2nd sc from beg 3 rows below, * sk next sc on working row, sc in next sc **, Ldc in 2nd sc from prev Ldc 3 rows below; rep from * across, ending last rep at **: 23 {25, 27, 29, 31, 33, 35} Ldc.
Row 7: Rep row 3.
Row 8: With MC, ch 1, turn; sc in first 2 sc, FPdccl around 5th sc from beg 3 rows below, * sc in next 3 sc, FPdccl around 4th sc from prev FPdccl 3 rows below; rep from * across, sc in last 4 sc: 11 {12, 13, 14, 15, 16, 17} FPdccl.

Rows 9 and 10: Rep rows 5 and 6.
Rows 11–76 [petite only]: Rep rows 3–10, 8 times, then rep rows 3 and 4 once; fasten off after last row.
Rows 11–80 [small, medium, and large only]: Rep rows 3–10, 8 times, then rep rows 3–8 once; fasten off after last row.
Rows 11–84 [extra-large, extra-extra-large, and extra-extra-extra-large only]: Rep rows 3–10, 9 times, then rep rows 3 and 4 once; fasten off after last row.

Front *(Make 2.)*
With MC, ch 32 {36, 36, 40, 44, 44, 48} loosely.
Work as for Back.

Assembly
Join 1 Front to Back as foll: with

rs facing and top edges aligned, join MC in top outer corner with sl st, ch 1, sc in first 16 {17, 18, 18, 20, 22, 24} sts. Rep with rem Front: 15 {17, 19, 23, 23, 23, 23} center sts of Back and 15 {18, 17, 21, 23, 21, 23} sts of ea Front unworked.
Mark bottom of Armholes 9¼" {10", 10", 11", 11", 11¾", 11¾"} from shoulder seams on Front and Back.

Sleeve *(Make 2.)*
Row 1 (ws): With ws facing, join MC at 1 Sleeve marker with sl st, ch 1, work 43 {47, 47, 51, 51, 55, 55} sc evenly across to next Sleeve marker, change to CC in last st.
Rows 2–4: Work as for Back.
Row 5: Ch 1, turn; dec in first 2 sts, sc in next st and in ea st across to last 2 sts, dec in last 2 sts, change to CC in last st: 41 {45, 45, 49, 49, 53, 53} sts.
Row 6: With CC, ch 1, turn; sc in first 2 sc, Ldc in 4th sc from beg 3 rows below, * sk next sc on working row, sc in next sc **, Ldc in 2nd sc from prev Ldc 3 rows below; rep from * across, ending last rep at **, sc in last sc: 19 {21, 21, 23, 23, 25, 25} Ldc.
Row 7: Ch 1, turn; sc in first sc and in ea st across, change to MC in last st.
Row 8: With MC, ch 1, turn; sc in first sc, FPdccl around 4th sc from beg 3 rows below, * sc in next 3 sc **, FPdccl around 4th sc from prev FPdccl 3 rows below; rep from * across, ending last rep at **: 10 {11, 11, 12, 12, 13, 13} FPdccl.
Row 9: Rep row 5: 39 {43, 43, 47, 47, 51, 51} sts.
Row 10: With CC, ch 1, turn; sc in first sc, Ldc in 3rd sc from beg 3 rows below, * sk next sc on

(Continued on page 114)

working row, sc in next sc **, Ldc in 2nd sc from prev Ldc 3 rows below; rep from * across, ending last rep at **: 19 {21, 21, 23, 23, 25, 25} Ldc.

Row 11: Rep row 7.

Row 12: With MC, ch 1, turn; sc in first 6 sc, FPdccl around 5th sc from beg 3 rows below, * sc in next 3 sc **, FPdccl around 4th sc from prev FPdccl 3 rows below; rep from * across, ending last rep at **, sc in last sc: 8 {9, 9, 10, 10, 11, 11} FPdccl.

Row 13: Rep row 5: 37 {41, 41, 45, 45, 49, 49} sts.

Row 14: Rep row 6: 17 {19, 19, 21, 21, 23, 23} Ldc.

Row 15: Rep row 7.

Row 16: With MC, ch 1, turn; sc in first 3 sc, FPdccl around 6th sc 3 rows below, * sc in next 3 sc **, FPdccl around 4th sc from prev FPdccl 3 rows below; rep from * across, ending last rep at **, sc in last 2 sc: 8 {9, 9, 10, 10, 11, 11} FPdccl.

Row 17: Rep row 5: 35 {39, 39, 43, 43, 47, 47} sts.

Row 18: Rep row 10: 17 {19, 19, 21, 21, 23, 23} Ldc.

Row 19: Rep row 11.

Row 20: With MC, ch 1, turn; sc in first 4 sc, FPdccl around 3rd sc from beg 3 rows below, * sc in next 3 sc, FPdccl around 4th sc from prev FPdccl 3 rows below; rep from * across, sc in last 2 sc: 8 {9, 9, 10, 10, 11, 11} FPdccl.

Row 21: Rep row 5: 33 {37, 37, 41, 41, 45, 45} sts.

Rows 22–49 {22–49, 22–45, 22–42} [sizes petite, small, medium, and extra-large only]: Rep rows 6–21 once, then rep rows 6–17 {6–17, 6–13, 6–10} once: 19 {23, 25, 31} sts.

Rows 22–37 [large only]: Rep rows 6–21 once: {33} sts.

Rows 22–25 [sizes extra-large and extra-extra-large only]: Rep rows 6–9 once {43, 43} sts.

Rows 50–68 {50–68} [sizes petite and small only]: Rep row 6 of Back once, then rep rows 3–10 of Back twice, then rep rows 3 and 4 of Back once; fasten off.

Rows 46–64 [size medium only]: Rep row 6 once, then rep row 5 once, then rep rows 8–10 of Back once, then rep rows 3–10 of Back once, then rep rows 3–8 of Back once; fasten off.

Rows 38–64 [size large only]: Rep rows 6–14 once, dec at ea end of ea odd row, rep row 5, then rep rows 8–10 of Back once, then rep rows 3–10 of Back once, then rep rows 3–8 of Back once; fasten off.

Rows 43–60 [size extra-large only]: Rep row 5 once, then rep rows 12–14 once, then rep rows 3–10 of Back once, then rep rows 3–8 of Back once; fasten off.

Rows 26–60 [sizes extra-extra-large and extra-extra-extra-large only]: Rep rows 6–21 once, dec at ea end of ea odd row, then rep rows 6–10 of Back once, then rep rows 3–10 of Back once, then rep rows 3–8 of Back once; fasten off.

Assembly

With rs tog and MC, sc side seams and Sleeve seams tog.

Edging

Rnd 1 (rs): With rs facing, join MC in any corner with sl st, ch 1, * 3 sc in same corner, sc evenly across to next corner; rep from * around; join with sl st to beg sc; fasten off.

Rnd 2 (ws): With ws facing, join CC in any corner with sl st, sl st in ea sc around; join with sl st to beg sl st; fasten off.

Belt

With MC, ch 164 {168, 172, 176, 180, 184, 188} loosely.
Work as for Back for 8 rows.
Edging
Work as for Edging for Jacket.

Project was stitched by Joann Moss with Jiffy: Mulberry #190 and Homespun: Modern #305.

Aran Sampler

Showcase several stitch patterns in one stunning afghan. Choose cream yarn for a traditional look or use two colors for a modern twist.

Materials

Worsted-weight wool yarn, approximately:
72 oz. (4,185 yd.) cream
Size J crochet hook or size to obtain gauge

Finished Size

Approximately 54" x 57"

Gauge

In pat, 14 sts and 15 rows = 4"

Gauge Swatch (Multiple of 4 sts + 2)

Ch 22. Work in pat for 20 rows.

Pattern Stitches

Long double crochet [Ldc]: Yo, insert hook from front to back in st indicated, yo and pull up long lp, (yo and pull through 2 lps) twice.

Front Post double crochet decrease [FPdc-dec]: Yo, insert hook from front to back around post of st indicated, yo and pull up lp, yo and pull through 2 lps, yo, insert hook from front to back around next st indicated, yo and pull up lp, yo and pull through 2 lps, yo and pull through all 3 lps on hook.

Front Post double crochet [FPdc]: Yo, insert hook from front to back around post of st indicated, yo and pull up lp, (yo and pull through 2 lps) twice.

Front Post triple crochet [FPtr]: Yo twice, insert hook from front to back around post of st indicated, yo and pull up lp, (yo and pull through 2 lps) 3 times.

Ch 190 loosely.

Row 1 (ws): Sc in 2nd ch from hook and in ea ch across: 189 sc.

Row 2 (rs): Ch 1, turn; sc in first sc and in ea sc across.

Row 3 and all Odd Rows: Ch 1, turn; sc in first sc and in ea st across.

Row 4: Ch 1, turn; sc in first sc, Ldc in 4th sc from beg 3 rows below, * sk next sc on working row, sc in next sc, Ldc in 2nd sc before prev Ldc 3 rows below [X-st made], sk next sc on working row, sc in next sc **, Ldc in 4th sc from prev Ldc 3 rows below; rep from * across, ending last rep at **: 47 X-sts.

Row 6: Ch 1, turn; sc in first 4 sc, sk first Ldc 3 rows below, * FPdc-dec around next 2 Ldc 3 rows below, sk next sc on working row, sc in next 3 sc **; rep from * across, ending last rep at **, sc in last sc: 46 FPdc-dec.

Rows 7–25: Rep rows 3–6, 4 times, then rep rows 3–5 once.

Row 26: Ch 1, turn; sc in first sc, FPdc around first Ldc 3 rows below, * sk next sc on working row, sc in next sc **, sk next Ldc 3 rows below, FPtr around next Ldc 3 rows below, sk next sc on working row, sc in next sc, FPtr around sk Ldc 3 rows below [X-st made]; rep from * across, ending last rep at **, FPdc around last Ldc 3 rows below, sk next sc on working row, sc in last sc: 46 X-sts and 2 FPdc.

Row 28: Ch 1, turn; sc in first sc, sk first FPdc 3 rows below, FPtr around first FPtr 3 rows below, sk next sc on working row, sc in next sc, FPtr around sk FPdc 3 rows below [X-st made], * sk next sc on working row, sc in next sc, sk next FPtr 3 rows below **, FPtr around next FPtr 3 rows below, sk next sc on working row, sc in next sc, FPtr around sk FPtr 3 rows below [X-st made]; rep from * across, ending last rep at **, FPtr around last FPdc 3 rows below, sk next sc on working row, sc in next sc, FPtr around sk FPtr 3 rows below [X-st made], sk next sc on working row, sc in last sc: 47 X-sts.

Row 30: Ch 1, turn; sc in first sc, FPdc around first FPtr 3 rows below, * sk next sc on working row, sc in next sc **, sk next FPtr 3 rows below, FPtr around next FPtr 3 rows below, sk next sc on working row, sc in next sc, FPtr around sk FPtr 3 rows below [X-st made]; rep from * across, ending last rep at **, FPdc around last FPtr 3 rows below, sk next sc on working row, sc in last sc: 46 X-sts and 2 FPdc.

Rows 32–37: Rep rows 28–31 once, then rep rows 28 and 29 once.

Row 38: Ch 1, turn; sc in first sc, FPdc around first FPtr 3 rows below, * sk next sc on working row, sc in next sc **, FPdc around next FPtr 3 rows below; rep from * across, ending last rep at **: 94 FPdc.

Row 40: Ch 1, turn; sc in first sc, sk first FPdc 3 rows below, * FPtr around next FPdc 3 rows below, sk next sc on working row, sc in next sc, FPtr around sk FPdc 3 rows below [X-st made], sk next sc on working row, sc in next sc **, sk next FPdc 3 rows below; rep from * across, ending last rep at **: 47 X-sts.

Rows 42–51: Rep rows 38–41, twice, then rep rows 38 and 39 once.

Row 52: Ch 1, turn; sc in first sc, FPdc around first FPdc 3 rows below, * sk next sc on working row, sc in next sc **, sk next FPdc 3 rows below, FPtr around next FPdc 3 rows below, sk next sc on working row, sc in next sc, FPtr around sk FPdc 3 rows below [X-st made]; rep from * across, ending last rep at **, FPdc around last Fdc 3 rows below, sk next sc on working row, sc in last sc: 46 X-sts and 2 FPdc.

Row 54: Ch 1, turn; sc in first sc, FPdc around first FPdc 3 rows below, * sk next sc on working row, sc in next sc **, FPdc around next FPtr 3 rows below; rep from * across, ending last rep at **, FPdc around last FPdc 3 rows below, sk next sc on working row: 94 FPdc.

Row 56: Rep row 40.

Row 58: Rep row 38.

Rows 60–73: Rep rows 52–59 once, then rep rows 52–57 once.

Row 74: Ch 1, turn; sc in first 2 sc, Ldc in 3rd sc from beg 3 rows below, * sk next sc on working row, sc in next sc **, FPdc-dec around next 2 FPtr 3 rows below, sk next sc on working row, sc in next sc, Ldc in 4th sc from prev Ldc 3 rows below; rep from * across, ending last rep at **, sc in last sc: 47 Ldc and 46 FPdc-dec.

Row 76: Ch 1, turn; sc in first sc, * FPdc around next Ldc 3 rows below, sk next sc on working row, sc in next sc, FPdc around same Ldc 3 rows below [V-st made], sk next sc on working row, sc in next sc; rep from * across: 47 V-sts.

Row 78: Ch 1, turn; sc in first 2 sc, Ldc in 3rd sc from beg 3 rows below, * sk next sc on working row, sc in next sc **, FPdc-dec around next 2 FPdc 3 rows below, sk next sc on working row, sc in

next sc, Ldc in 4th sc from prev Ldc 3 rows below; rep from * across, ending last rep at **, sc in last sc: 47 Ldc and 46 FPdc-dec.

Rows 80–87: Rep rows 76–79 twice.

Row 88: Ch 1, turn; sc in first 3 sc, Ldc in 6th sc from beg 3 rows below, * sk next sc on working row, sc in next sc, Ldc in 2nd sc before prev Ldc 3 rows below [X-st made], sk next sc on working row, sc in next sc **, Ldc in 4th sc from prev Ldc 3 rows below; rep from * across, ending last rep at **, sc in last 2 sc: 46 X-sts.

Row 90: Ch 1, turn; sc in first 2 sc, FPtr around first Ldc 3 rows below, * sk next sc on working row, sc in next 3 sc **, FPdc-dec around next 2 Ldc 3 rows below; rep from * across, ending last rep at **, FPtr around last Ldc 3 rows below, sk next sc on working row, sc in last 2 sc: 45 FPdc-dec and 2 FPtr.

Rows 92–95: Rep rows 4–7 once.

Rows 96–109: Rep rows 88–95 once, then rep rows 88–93 once.

Row 110: Ch 1, turn; sc in first sc, FPdc around first Ldc 3 rows below, * sk next sc on working row, sc in next sc **, FPdc around next Ldc 3 rows below; rep from

* across, ending last rep at **: 94 FPdc.

Row 112: Rep row 40.

Row 114: Rep row 38.

Rows 116–123: Rep rows 112–115 twice.

Rows 124–127: Rep rows 52–55.

Rows 128–139: Rep rows 124–127, 3 times.

Rows 140–153: Rep rows 112–115, 3 times, then rep rows 112 and 113 once.

Row 154: Rep row 30.

Row 156: Rep row 28.

Rows 158–165: Rep rows 154–157, twice.

Row 166: Ch 1, turn; sc in first 4 sc, sk first FPtr 3 rows below, * FPdc-dec around next 2 FPtr 3 rows below, sk next sc on working row, sc in next 3 sc **; rep from * across, ending last rep at **, sc in last sc: 46 FPdc-dec.

Rows 168–187: Rep rows 4–7, 5 times.

Row 188: Ch 1, turn; sc in first 2 sc, Ldc in 3rd sc from beg 3 rows below, * sk next sc on working row **, sc in next 3 sc, Ldc in 4th sc from prev Ldc 3 rows below; rep from * across, ending last rep at **, sc in last 2 sc: 47 Ldc.

Rows 190–193: Rep rows 76–79.

Rows 194–213: Rep rows 190–193, 5 times; do not turn after last row; do not fasten off.

Border

Rnd 1 (ws): With ws facing, ch 1, sc in last st, sc evenly across to next corner, 3 sc in corner, sc in ea ch across to next corner, 3 sc in corner, sc evenly across to next corner, 3 sc in corner, sc in ea st across to next corner; join with sl st to beg sc.

Rnd 2 (rs): Turn; sl st in same st and in ea st around; join with sl st to beg sl st; fasten off.

Project was stitched by Marge Wild with Fishermen's Wool: Natural #098.

Striped Sampler

Materials

Worsted-weight wool-blend yarn, approximately:
39 oz. (2,565 yd.) blue, MC
30 oz. (1,970 yd.) gray, CC
Size J crochet hook or size to obtain gauge

Note: *To change colors, work last yo of prev st with new color, dropping prev color to ws of work. Do not fasten off when changing colors.*

Color sequence: *1 row MC, (2 rows CC, 2 rows MC) throughout, ending with 1 row MC.*

Work as for Aran Sampler, foll color sequence.

Note: *Work Border with MC.*

Project was stitched by Peggy Stiver with Wool-ease: Blue Mist #115 and Slate Heather #108.

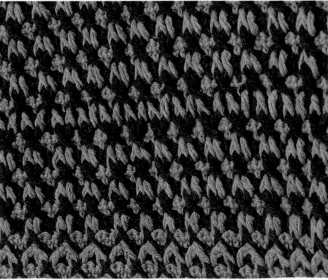

Herringbone

Bring high fashion to your home with an afghan reminiscent of a classic Chanel suit. A wide border with shell-stitch edging is the finishing touch.

Materials
Worsted-weight chenille yarn,
approximately:
35 oz. (2,175 yd.) red, MC
28 oz. (1,740 yd.) black, CC
Sizes G and H crochet hooks
or sizes to obtain gauge

Finished Size
Approximately 57" x 64", without
border

Gauge
In pat with larger hook, 10 sts
and 12 rows = 3"

Gauge Swatch (Multiple
of 4 sts)
With larger hook and CC, ch 20.
Work in pat for 20 rows.

Pattern Stitch
Long double crochet [Ldc]: Yo,
insert hook from front to back in
st indicated, yo and pull up long
lp, (yo and pull through 2 lps)
twice.

*Note: To change colors, work
last yo of prev st with new color,
dropping prev color to ws of
work. Do not fasten off when
changing colors.*

With larger hook and CC, ch 160
loosely.

Row 1 (rs): Sc in 2nd ch from
hook and in ea ch across; change
to MC in last st: 159 sc.

Row 2 (ws): With MC, ch 1,
turn; sc in first sc and in ea sc
across.

Row 3: Ch 1, turn; sc in first sc
and in ea st across; change to CC
in last st; ch 1, turn.

Row 4: With CC, sc in first sc,
Ldc in 4th sc from beg 3 rows
below [slant-st made], * sk next
sc on working row, sc in next
3 sc **, Ldc in 4th sc from prev
Ldc 3 rows below [slant st made];
rep from * across, ending last rep

at **, sc in last 2 sc: 39 slant-sts.

Row 5: Ch 1, turn; sc in first sc and in ea st across; change to MC in last st.

Row 6: With MC, ch 1, turn; sc in first 5 sc, Ldc in 4th sc from beg 3 rows below [slant-st made], * sk next sc on working row **, sc in next 3 sc, Ldc in 4th sc from prev Ldc 3 rows below [slant-st made]; rep from * across, ending last rep at **, sc in last sc: 39 slant-sts.

Rows 7–220: Rep rows 3–6, 53 times, then rep rows 3 and 4 once; fasten off.

Border

Note: *To work 181 sc evenly across side edges, * work 1 sc in ends of ea of 5 rows, sk next row, sc in ends of ea of next 4 rows; rep from * to corner.*

Rnd 1 (rs): With rs facing and larger hook, join MC in top right corner with sl st, ch 1, sc in same st and in ea st across to next corner [157 sc], 3 sc in corner, work 181 sc evenly across to next corner, 3 sc in corner, sc in ea ch across to next corner [157 sc], 3 sc in corner, work 181 sc evenly across to next corner, 2 sc in corner; join with sl st to beg sc: 688 sc.

Note: *Change to smaller hook.*

Rnd 2 (ws): With smaller hook, ch 4, turn; (2 dc, ch 1, 2 dc) in same corner, * sk next 3 sc, [(2 dc, ch 1, 2 dc) in next sc [shell st made], sk next 3 sc] across to corner **, (2 dc, ch 1, 2 dc, ch 1, 2 dc) in corner; rep from * around, ending last rep at **, dc in corner; join with sl st to 3rd ch of beg ch-4: 168 shell sts.

Rnd 3 (ws): Sl st in next ch-1 sp, (ch 3, dc, ch 1, 2 dc) in same ch-1 sp, shell st in ea ch-1 sp around; join with sl st to 3rd ch of beg ch-3.

Rnd 4 (ws): Sl st in next dc and in next ch-1 sp, (ch 3, dc, ch 1, 2 dc) in same ch-1 sp, sk 2 dc, shell st in sp before next 2 dc [corner sp], * shell st in ea ch-1 sp across to corner **, shell st in corner sp; rep from * around, ending last rep at **; join with sl st to 3rd ch of beg ch-3.

Rnd 5 (ws): Sl st in next dc and in next ch-1 sp, (ch 3, dc, ch 1, 2 dc) in same ch-1 sp, * (2 dc, ch 1, 2 dc, ch 1, 2 dc) in corner ch-1 sp, shell st in ea ch-1 sp across to next corner; rep from * around; join with sl st to 3rd ch of beg ch-3.

Rnd 6 (ws): Sl st in next dc and in next ch-1 sp, (ch 3, dc, ch 1, 2 dc) in same ch-1 sp, shell st in ea ch-1 sp around; join with sl st to 3rd ch of beg ch-3.

Rnd 7 (ws): Sl st in next dc and in next ch-1 sp, (ch 3, dc, ch 1, 2 dc) in same ch-1 sp, shell st in next ch-1 sp, sk next 2 dc, shell st in sp before next 2 dc [corner sp], * shell in ea ch-1 sp across to next corner **, shell st in corner sp; rep from * around, ending last rep at **; join with sl st to 3rd ch of beg ch-3; fasten off.

Rnd 8 (rs): With rs facing, join CC in any sp between 2 shell sts with sl st, ch 1, sc in same sp, * sk next 2 dc, 5 dc in next ch-1 sp, sk next 2 dc **, sc in sp before next shell st; rep from * around, ending last rep at **; join with sl st to beg sc; fasten off.

Project was stitched by Marge Scensny with Chenille Sensations: Red #112 and Black #153.

Black Lattice

The center of each diamond in this lattice pattern resembles a fleur-de-lis. Stitch it in purple and gold for a New Orleans-style Mardi Gras.

Materials

Worsted-weight alpaca-wool-acrylic-blend yarn, approximately:
2¾ oz. (1,395 yd.) gray, MC
2¾ oz. (1,395 yd.) black, CC
Size K crochet hook or size to obtain gauge

Finished Size

Approximately 49" x 57"

Gauge

In pat, 10 sts and 14 rows = 4"

Gauge Swatch *(Multiple of 4 sts + 2)*

With CC, ch 22. Work in pat for 20 rows.

Pattern Stitch

Long double crochet [Ldc]: Yo, insert hook from front to back in st indicated, yo and pull up long lp, (yo and pull through 2 lps) twice.

Note: *To change colors, work last yo of prev st with new color, dropping prev color to ws of work. Do not fasten off when changing colors.*

With CC, ch 122 loosely.
Row 1 (ws): Sc in 2nd ch from hook and in ea ch across, change to MC in last st: 121 sc.
Row 2 (rs): With MC, ch 1, turn; sc in first sc and in ea sc across.
Row 3: Ch 1, turn; sc in first sc and in ea st across, change to CC in last st.
Row 4: With CC, ch 1, turn; sc in first sc, Ldc in 4th sc from beg 3 rows below, * sk next sc on working row, sc in next sc, Ldc in 2nd sc before prev Ldc 3 rows below [X-st made], sk next sc on working row, sc in next sc **, Ldc in 4th sc from prev Ldc 3 rows below; rep from * across, ending last rep at **: 30 X-sts.
Row 5: Ch 1, turn; sc in first sc and in ea st across, change to MC in last st.
Row 6: With MC, ch 1, turn; sc in first 2 sc, Ldc in 3rd sc from beg 3 rows below, * sk next sc on working row, sc in next sc **, Ldc in 2nd sc from prev Ldc 3 rows below; rep from * across, ending last rep at **, sc in last sc: 59 Ldc.
Row 7: Rep row 3.
Row 8: With CC, ch 1, turn; sc in first 3 sc, Ldc in 6th sc from beg 3 rows below, * sk next sc on working row, sc in next sc, Ldc in 2nd sc before prev Ldc 3 rows below [X-st made], sk next sc on working row, sc in next sc **, Ldc in 4th sc from prev Ldc 3 rows below; rep from * across, ending last rep at **, sc in last 2 sc: 29 X-sts.
Rows 9 and 10: Rep rows 5 and 6 once.
Rows 11–196: Rep rows 3–10, 23 times, then rep rows 3 and 4 once; do not turn after last row; fasten off MC; do not fasten off CC.

Border

Rnd 1 (rs): With rs facing and CC, ch 1, 3sc in last st, sc evenly across to next corner, 3 sc in corner, sc in ea ch across to next corner, 3 sc in corner, sc evenly across to next corner, 3 sc in corner, sc in ea st across to next corner; join with sl st to beg sc.
Rnd 2 (rs): Ch 1, working from left to right [reverse sc], sc in ea sc around; join with sl st to beg sc; fasten off.

Tassels

For ea tassel, referring to page 143 of General Directions, wind yarn around 8" piece of cardboard 60 times. Join 1 MC tassel and 1 CC tassel to ea corner.

Project was stitched by Peggy Stiver with Al-Pa-Ka: Silver Grey #149 and Black #153.

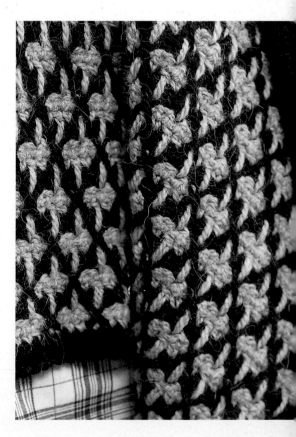

Fair Isle Fancy

Fair Isle stripes make beautiful afghans. Be sure to choose colors that contrast strongly.

Materials

Worsted-weight wool-blend yarn, approximately:
27 oz. (1,775 yd.) gray, MC
21 oz. (1,380 yd.) red, A
10 oz. (650 yd.) white, B
Size J crochet hook or size to obtain gauge

Finished Size

Approximately 54" x 58"

Gauge

In pat, 12 sts and 14 rows = 4"

Gauge Swatch *(Multiple of 8 sts + 6)*

With A, ch 22. Work in pat for 20 rows.

Pattern Stitch

Long double crochet [Ldc]: Yo, insert hook from front to back in st indicated, yo and pull up long lp, (yo and pull through 2 lps) twice.

Note: To change colors, work last yo of prev st with new color, dropping prev color to ws of work. Do not fasten off when changing colors.

*Color sequence: 1 row A, (2 rows MC, 2 rows A) twice, 2 rows MC, * (1 row A, 1 row B, 2 rows MC, 1 row B, 1 row A, 2 rows MC) 3 times **, (2 rows A, 2 rows MC) 6 times; rep from * 3 times, ending last rep at **, (2 rows A, 2 rows MC) twice, 1 row A.*

With A, ch 174 loosely.
Row 1 (ws): Sc in 2nd ch from hook and in ea ch across: 173 sc.
Row 2 (rs): Ch 1, turn; sc in first sc and in ea sc across.
Row 3 and all Odd Rows: Ch 1, turn; sc in first sc and in ea st across.
Row 4: Ch 1, turn; sc in first sc, Ldc in 4th sc from beg 3 rows below, * sk next sc on working row, sc in next sc, Ldc in 2nd sc before prev Ldc 3 rows below [X-st made], sk next sc on working row, sc in next sc **, (Ldc in 2nd sc from prev Ldc 3 rows below, sk next sc on working row, sc in next sc) twice, Ldc in 4th sc from prev Ldc 3 rows below; rep from * across, ending last rep at **: 22 X-sts and 42 Ldc.
Row 6: Ch 1, turn; sc in first 4 sc, Ldc in 5th sc from beg 3 rows below, * sk next sc on working row, sc in next 3 sc **, Ldc in 4th sc from prev Ldc 3 rows below; rep from * across, ending last rep at **, sc in last sc: 42 Ldc.
Row 8: Ch 1, turn; sc in first sc, Ldc in 2nd sc from beg 3 rows below, * sk next sc on working row, sc in next sc, Ldc in 2nd sc from prev Ldc 3 rows below, sk next sc on working row, sc in next sc **, Ldc in 4th sc from prev Ldc 3 rows below, sk next sc on working row, sc in next sc, Ldc in 2nd sc before prev Ldc 3 rows below [X-st made], sk next sc on working row, sc in next sc, Ldc in 2nd sc from prev Ldc 3 rows below; rep from * across, ending last rep at **: 21 X-sts and 44 Ldc.

Row 10: Rep row 6.
Rows 11–188: Rep rows 3–10, 22 times, then rep rows 3 and 4 once; do not turn after last row; fasten off MC and B after last row; do not fasten off A.

Border

Rnd 1 (rs): With rs facing and A, ch 1, 3 sc in last st, sc evenly across to next corner, 3 sc in corner, sc in ea ch across to next corner, 3 sc in corner, sc evenly across to next corner, 3 sc in corner, sc in ea sc across to next corner; join with sl st to beg sc; fasten off.
Rnd 2 (ws): With ws facing, join B in any corner with sl st, ch 1, 3 sc in same st, sc in ea sc across to next corner, * 3 sc in corner, sc in ea sc across to next corner; rep from * around; join with sl st to beg sc; fasten off.
Rnd 3 (rs): With rs facing, join MC in any corner with sl st, ch 1, * sc in ea sc across to next corner, 3 sc in corner rep from * around; join with sl st to beg sc.
Rnd 4 (rs): Ch 1, turn; working from left to right [reverse sc], sc in same sc and in ea sc around; join with sl st to beg sc; fasten off.

Project was stitched by Peggy Stiver with Wool-ease: Oxford Grey #152, Cranberry #138, and White Multi #301.

Fair Isle Pullover

Knitters aren't the only ones who can fashion this beautiful sweater style. Careful shaping and details, including the two-colored ribbing, make this an exacting project.

Materials
Worsted-weight wool-blend yarn, approximately:
15 {15, 15, 18, 21} oz. (985 {985; 985; 1,185; 1,380} yd.) blue, MC
15 {15, 15, 18, 21} oz. (985 {985; 985; 1,185; 1,380} yd.) black, A
3 {3, 3, 3, 6} oz. (200 {200, 200, 200, 395} yd.) cream, B
Sizes G and H crochet hooks or sizes to obtain gauge
Yarn needle

Note: *Directions are written for men's size small, with sizes medium, large, extra-large, and extra-extra-large in braces { }. Circle all numbers pertaining to desired size before beginning.*

Finished Size
Chest: 40½" {46", 51", 56½", 62"}
Length: 25" {25", 25", 27", 27"}

Gauge
In pat with larger hook, 12 sts and 16 rows = 4"

Gauge Swatch *(Multiple of 8 sts + 6)*
With MC ch 22.
Row 1: Sc in 2nd ch from hook and in ea ch across: 21 sc.
Rep rows 2–20 of Back.

Pattern Stitches
Long double crochet [Ldc]: Yo, insert hook from front to back in st indicated, yo and pull up long lp, (yo and pull through 2 lps) twice.
Decrease [dec]: [Worked over 2 sts] Insert hook in st indicated, yo and pull up lp, insert hook in next st, yo and pull up lp, yo and pull through all 3 lps on hook.

Note: Ribbing is worked from side to side, then Body is worked vertically on edge of Ribbing. To change colors, work last yo of prev st with new color, dropping prev color to ws of work. Do not fasten off when changing colors.

Back
Ribbing
With A and smaller hook, ch 13 loosely.
Row 1 (ws): Sc in 2nd ch from hook and in ea ch across, changing to MC in last st: 12 sc.
Row 2 (rs): With MC, ch 1, turn; sc in first sc, sc in bk lps only of next 10 sc, sc in both lps of last sc.
Row 3: Ch 1, turn; sc in first sc, sc in bk lps only of next 10 sc, sc in both lps of last sc, change to A in last st.
Row 4: With A, ch 1, turn; sc in first sc, sc in bk lps only of next 10 sc, sc in both lps of last sc.
Row 5: Ch 1, turn; sc in first sc, sc in bk lps only of next 10 sc, sc in both lps of last sc, change to MC in last st.
Rows 6–60 {6–68, 6–76, 6–84, 6–92}: Rep rows 2–5, 13 {15, 17, 19, 21} times, then rep rows 2–4 once; fasten off.

Body
Color sequence: *(2 rows MC, 2 rows A) 12 {12, 12, 14, 14} times, (1 row MC, 1 row B, 2 rows A, 1 row B, fasten off B, 1 row MC, 2 rows A) 3 times, (2 rows MC, 2 rows A) 4 times, 1 row MC.*

Row 1 (ws): With rs facing and larger hook, join MC in bottom right corner of Ribbing with sl st, ch 1, work 61 {69, 77, 85, 93} sc evenly across side edge of Ribbing.
Row 2 and all Even Rows (rs): Ch 1, turn; sc in first sc and in ea st across.
Row 3: Ch 1, turn; sc in first sc and in ea st across.
Row 5: Ch 1, turn; sc in first sc, Ldc in 4th sc from beg 3 rows below, * sk next sc on working row, sc in next sc, sc in 2nd sc before prev Ldc 3 rows below [X-st made] **, (sk next sc on working row, sc in next sc, Ldc in 2nd sc from prev Ldc 3 rows below) twice, sk next sc, sc in next sc, Ldc in 4th sc from prev Ldc 3 rows below; rep from * across, ending last rep at **, sk next sc on working row, sc in last sc: 8 {9, 10, 11, 12} X-sts.
Row 7: Ch 1, turn; sc in first 4 sc, Ldc in 5th sc from beg 3 rows below, * sk next sc on working row, sc in next 3 sc **, Ldc in 4th sc from prev Ldc 3 rows below; rep from * across, ending last rep at **, sc in last sc: 14 {16, 18, 20, 22} Ldc.

(Continued on page 128)

Row 9: Ch 1, turn; sc in first sc, Ldc in 2nd sc from beg 3 rows below, * sk next sc on working row, sc in next sc, Ldc in 2nd sc from prev Ldc 3 rows below, sk next sc on working row, sc in next sc **, Ldc in 4th sc from prev Ldc 3 rows below, sk next sc on working row, sc in next sc, Ldc in 2nd sc before prev Ldc 3 rows below [X-st made], sk next sc on working row, sc in next sc, Ldc in 2nd sc from prev Ldc 3 rows below; rep from * across, ending last rep at **: 7 {8, 9, 10, 11} X-sts.

Row 11: Rep row 7.

Rows 12–89 {12–89, 12–89, 12–97, 12–97}: Rep rows 4–11, 9 {9, 9, 10, 10} times, then rep rows 4–9 once; fasten off after last row.

Front

Work as for Back for 77 {77, 77, 85, 85} rows, foll color sequence; do not fasten off.

Right Neck Shaping
Note: *Cont color sequence as for Back.*

Row 1 (ws): Ch 1, turn; sc in first 26 {30, 34, 38, 42} sc.

Row 2 (rs): Ch 1, turn; dec in first 2 sts, sc in next 3 sc, Ldc in sc 3 rows below next sc, * sk next sc on working row, sc in next 3 sc **, Ldc in 4th sc from prev Ldc 3 rows below; rep from * across ending last rep at **, sc in last sc: 5 {6, 7, 8, 9} Ldc.

Row 3: Ch 1, turn; sc in ea st across to last 2 sc, dec in last 2 sc: 24 {28, 32, 36, 40} sts.

Row 4 [sizes small, large, and extra-extra-large]: Ch 1, turn; dec in first 2 sts, sc in next 2 sc, Ldc in sc 3 rows below next sc, * sk next sc on working row, sc in next sc, Ldc in 2nd sc from prev Ldc 3 rows below, sk next sc on working row, sc in next sc **,

work X-st over next 3 sts, sk next sc on working row, sc in next sc, Ldc in 2nd sc from prev Ldc 3 rows below; rep from * across, ending last rep at **: 2 {3, 4} X-sts.

Row 4 [sizes medium and extra-large]: Ch 1, turn; dec in first 2 sts, sc in next 2 sc, * work X-st over next 3 sts, sk next sc on working row, sc in next sc, (Ldc in 2nd sc from prev Ldc 3 rows below, sk next sc on working row, sc in next sc) twice; rep from * across: {3, 4} X-sts.

Row 5 [all sizes]: Rep row 3: 22 {26, 30, 34, 38} sts.

Rows 6 and 7 [all sizes]: Rep rows 2 and 3 once: 20 {24, 28, 32, 36} sts.

Row 8 [sizes small, large, and extra-extra-large]: Ch 1, turn; sc in first 4 sts, Ldc in sc 3 rows below next sc, * sk next sc on working row, sc in next sc, Ldc in 2nd sc from prev Ldc 3 rows below, sk next sc on working row, sc in next sc **, work X-st over next 3 sts, sk next sc on working row, sc in next sc, Ldc in 2nd sc from prev Ldc 3 rows below; rep from * across, ending last rep at **: 2 {3, 4} X-sts.

Row 8 [sizes medium and extra-large]: Ch 1, turn; sc in first 4 sts, * work X-st over next 3 sts, sk next sc on working row, sc in next sc **, (Ldc in 2nd sc from prev Ldc 3 rows below, sk next sc on working row, sc in next sc) twice; rep from * across, ending last rep at **: {3, 4} X-sts.

Row 9 [all sizes]: Rep row 3: 19 {23, 27, 31, 35} sts.

Row 10 [all sizes]: Ch 1, turn; sc in first 2 sts, Ldc in sc 3 rows below next sc, * sk next sc on working row, sc in next 3 sc **, Ldc in 4th sc from prev Ldc 3 rows below; rep from * across ending last rep at **, sc in last sc: 4 {5, 6, 7, 8} Ldc.

Row 11 [all sizes]: Rep row 3: 18 {22, 26, 30, 34} sts.

Row 12 [sizes small, large, and extra-extra-large]: Ch 1, turn; sc in first 2 sc, * work X-st over next 3 sts, sk next sc on working row, sc in next sc, (Ldc in 2nd sc from prev Ldc 3 rows below, sk next sc on working row, sc in next sc) twice; rep from * across; fasten off: 2 {3, 4} X-sts.

Row 12 [sizes medium and extra-large]: Ch 1, turn; sc in first 2 sc, Ldc in sc 3 rows below next sc * sk next sc on working row, sc in next sc, Ldc in 2nd sc from prev Ldc 3 rows below, sk next sc on working row, sc in next sc **, work X-st over next 3 sts, sk next sc on working row, sc in next sc, Ldc in 2nd sc from prev Ldc 3 rows below; rep from * across, ending last rep at **; fasten off: {2, 3} X-sts.

Left Neck Shaping
Note: *Cont color sequence as for Back.*

Row 1 (ws): With ws facing and larger hook, sk 9 sts on Front and join MC in 10th sc from last sc on row 1 of Right Neck Shaping with sl st, ch 1, sc in same st and in ea rem st across: 26 {30, 34, 38, 42} sc.

Row 2 (rs): Ch 1, turn; sc in first 4 sc, Ldc in 5th sc from beg 3 rows below, * sk next sc on working row, sc in next 3 sc **, Ldc in 4th sc from prev Ldc 3 rows below; rep from * across, ending last rep at **, dec in last 2 sc: 5 {6, 7, 8, 9} Ldc.

Row 3: Ch 1, turn; dec in first 2 sc, sc in ea st across: 24 {28, 32, 36, 40} sts.

Row 4 [sizes small, large, and extra-extra-large]: Ch 1, turn; sc in first sc, Ldc in 2nd sc from beg 3 rows below, * sk next sc on working row, sc in next sc, Ldc in 2nd sc from prev Ldc 3 rows

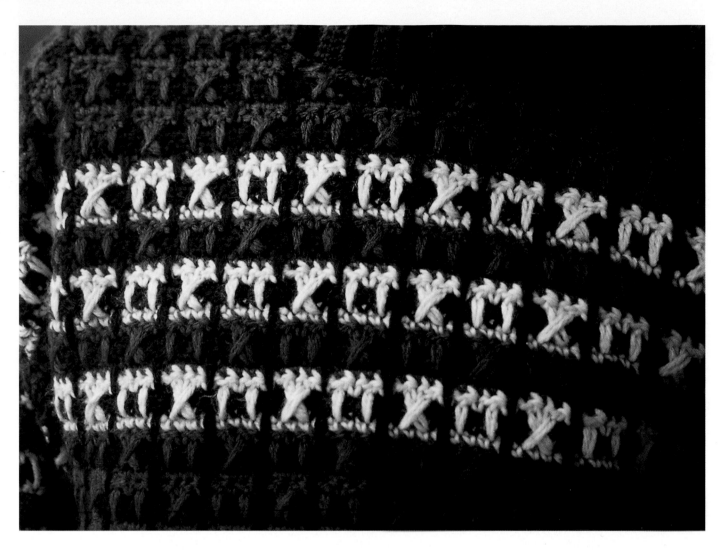

below, sk next sc on working row, sc in next sc **, work X-st over next 3 sts, sk next sc on working row, sc in next sc, Ldc in 2nd sc from prev Ldc 3 rows below; rep from * across, ending last rep at **, sc in next 2 sc, dec in last 2 sc: 2 {3, 4} X-sts.

Row 4 [sizes medium and extra-large]: Ch 1, turn; sc in first sc, Ldc in 2nd sc from beg 3 rows below, * sk next sc on working row, sc in next sc, Ldc in 2nd sc from prev Ldc 3 rows below, sk next sc on working row, sc in next sc, work X-st over next 3 sts, sk next sc on working row, sc in next sc **, Ldc in 2nd sc from prev Ldc 3 rows below; rep from * across, ending last rep at **, sc in next sc, dec in last 2 sc: {3, 4} X-sts.

Row 5 [all sizes]: Rep row 3: 22 {26, 30, 34, 38} sts.

Rows 6 and 7 [all sizes]: Rep rows 2 and 3 once: 20 {24, 28, 32, 36} sts.

Row 8 [sizes small, large, and extra-extra-large]: Ch 1, turn; sc in first sc, * work X-st over next 3 sts, (sk next sc on working row, sc in next sc, Ldc in 2nd sc from prev Ldc 3 rows below) twice, sk next sc on working row, sc in next sc **; rep from * across, ending last rep at **, sc in last 3 sts: 2 {3, 4} X-sts.

Row 8 [sizes medium and extra-large]: Ch 1, turn; sc in first sc, * work X-st over next 3 sts **, (sk next sc on working row, sc in next sc, Ldc in 2nd sc from prev Ldc 3 rows below) twice, sk next sc on working row,

se in next sc; rep from * across, ending last rep at **, sc in last 4 sts: {3, 4} X-sts.

Row 9 [all sizes]: Rep row 3: 19 {23, 27, 31, 35} sts.

Row 10 [all sizes]: Ch 1, turn; sc in first 4 sc, Ldc in 5th sc from beg 3 rows below, * sk next sc on working row **, sc in next 3 sc, Ldc in 4th sc from prev Ldc 3 rows below; rep from * across, ending last rep at **, sc in last 2 sc: 4 {5, 6, 7, 8} Ldc.

Row 11 [all sizes]: Rep row 3: 18 {22, 26, 30, 34} sts.

Row 12 [sizes small, large, and extra-extra-large]: Ch 1, turn; sc in first sc, Ldc in 2nd sc from beg 3 rows below, * sk next sc on working row, sc in next sc,

(Continued on page 130)

Ldc in 2nd sc from prev Ldc 3 rows below, sk next sc on working row, sc in next sc, work X-st over next 3 sts, sk next sc on working row, sc in next sc **, Ldc in 2nd sc from prev Ldc 3 rows below; rep from * across, ending last rep at **, sc in last sc; fasten off: 2 {3, 4} X-sts.

Row 12 [sizes medium and extra-large]: Ch 1, turn; sc in first sc, Ldc in 2nd sc from beg 3 rows below, * sk next sc on working row, sc in next sc, Ldc in 2nd sc from prev Ldc 3 rows below, sk next sc on working row, sc in next sc **, work X-st over next 3 sts, sk next sc on working row, sc in next sc, Ldc in 2nd sc from prev Ldc 3 rows below; rep from * across, ending last rep at **, sc in last sc; fasten off: {2, 3} X-sts.

Small Sleeve (Make 2.)
Ribbing
With A and smaller hook, ch 9 loosely.
Work as for Back Ribbing for 28 rows; fasten off after last row.
Body
Color sequence: (2 rows MC, 2 rows A) 11 times, (1 row MC, 1 row B, 2 rows A, 1 row B, fasten off B, 1 row MC, 2 rows A) 3 times, 1 row MC.

Row 1 (rs): With rs facing and larger hook, join MC in bottom right corner of Ribbing with sl st, ch 1, work 29 sc evenly across side edge of Ribbing.
Rows 2–4: Ch 1, turn; sc in first sc and in ea st across.
Row 5: Rep row 5 of Back: 4 X-sts and 6 Ldc.
Row 6: Ch 1, turn; 2 sc in first sc, sc in next sc and in ea sc across to last sc, 2 sc in last sc: 31 sc.
Row 7: Ch 1, turn; sc in first sc, Ldc in first sc 3 rows below, * sk next sc on working row **,

sc in next 3 sc, Ldc in 4th sc from prev Ldc 3 rows below; rep from * across, ending last rep at **, sc in last sc: 8 Ldc.
Row 8: Rep row 2: 31 sc.
Row 9: Ch 1, turn; sc in first 2 sc, Ldc in 3rd sc from beg 3 rows below, * sk next sc on working row, sc in next sc, Ldc in 2nd sc from prev Ldc 3 rows below, sk next sc on working row, sc in next sc **, work X-st over next 3 sts, sk next sc on working row, sc in next sc, Ldc in 2nd sc from prev Ldc 3 rows below; rep from * across, ending last rep at **, sc in last sc: 3 X-sts and 8 Ldc.
Row 10: Rep row 6: 33 sc.
Row 11: Ch 1, turn; sc in first 2 sc, Ldc in 2nd sc from beg 3 rows below, * sk next sc on working row **, sc in next 3 sc, Ldc in 4th sc from prev Ldc 3 rows below; rep from * across, ending last rep at **, sc in last 2 sc: 8 Ldc.
Row 12: Rep row 2: 33 sc.
Row 13: Ch 1, turn; sc in first 3 sc, * work X-st over next 3 sts, sk next sc on working row, sc in next sc **, (Ldc in 2nd sc from prev Ldc 3 rows below, sk next sc on working row, sc in next sc) twice; rep from * across, ending last rep at **, sc in last 2 sc: 4 X-sts and 6 Ldc.
Row 14: Rep row 6: 35 sc.
Row 15: Ch 1, turn; sc in first 3 sc, Ldc in 3rd sc from beg 3 rows below, * sk next sc on working row, sc in next 3 sc **, Ldc in 4th sc from prev Ldc 3 rows below; rep from * across, ending last rep at **: 8 Ldc.
Row 16: Rep row 2: 35 sc.
Row 17: Ch 1, turn; sc in first 4 sc, Ldc in 5th sc from beg 3 rows below, * sk next sc on working row, sc in next sc, Ldc in 2nd sc from prev Ldc 3 rows below, sk next sc on working row, sc in next sc **, work X-st over next 3 sts, sk next sc on working row,

sc in next sc, Ldc in 2nd sc from prev Ldc 3 rows below; rep from * across, ending last rep at **, sc in last 3 sc: 3 X-sts and 8 Ldc.
Row 18: Rep row 6: 37 sc.
Row 19: Ch 1, turn; sc in first 4 sc, Ldc in 4th sc from beg 3 rows below, * sk next sc on working row, sc in next 3 sc **, Ldc in 4th sc from prev Ldc 3 rows below; rep from * across, ending last rep at **, sc in last sc: 8 Ldc.
Row 20: Rep row 2: 37 sc.
Row 21: Rep row 9 of Back: 4 X-sts and 10 Ldc.
Rows 22–24: Rep rows 6–8 once: 39 sc.
Row 25: Ch 1, turn; sc in first 2 sc, * work X-st over next 3 sts, sk next sc on working row, sc in next sc **, (Ldc in 2nd sc from prev Ldc 3 rows below, sk next sc on working row, sc in next sc) twice; rep from * across, ending last rep at **, sk next sc on working row, sc in last sc: 5 X-sts and 8 Ldc.
Row 26: Rep row 2: 39 sc.
Row 27: Ch 1, turn; sc in first sc, Ldc in 2nd sc from beg 3 rows below, * sk next sc on working row **, sc in next 3 sc, Ldc in 4th sc from prev Ldc 3 rows below; rep from * across, ending last rep at **, sc in last sc: 10 Ldc.
Row 28: Rep row 6: 41 sc.
Row 29: Ch 1, turn; sc in first 3 sc, Ldc in 3rd sc from beg 3 rows below, * sk next sc on working row, sc in next sc, Ldc in 2nd sc from prev Ldc 3 rows below, sk next sc on working row, sc in next sc **, work X-st over next 3 sts, sk next sc on working row, sc in next sc, Ldc in 2nd sc from prev Ldc 3 rows below; rep from * across, ending last rep at **, sc in last 2 sc: 4 X-sts and 10 Ldc.
Row 30: Rep row 2: 41 sc.
Row 31: Ch 1, turn; sc in first 2 sc, Ldc in 3rd sc from beg 3 rows below, * sk next sc on

working row **, sc in next 3 sc, Ldc in 4th sc from prev Ldc 3 rows below; rep from * across, ending last rep at **, sc in last 2 sc: 10 Ldc.

Rows 32–37: Rep rows 12–17 once: 4 X-sts and 10 Ldc.

Row 38: Rep row 2: 43 sc.

Row 39: Ch 1, turn; sc in first 3 sc, Ldc in 4th sc from beg 3 rows below, * sk next sc on working row, sc in next 3 sc **, Ldc in 4th sc from prev Ldc 3 rows below; rep from * across, ending last rep at **: 10 Ldc.

Row 40: Rep row 6: 45 sc.

Row 41: Ch 1, turn; sc in first sc, Ldc in first sc 3 rows below, * sk next sc on working row, sc in next sc, Ldc in 2nd sc from prev Ldc 3 rows below, sk next sc on working row, sc in next sc **, work X-st over next 3 sts, sk next sc on working row, sc in next sc, Ldc in 2nd sc from prev Ldc 3 rows below; rep from * across, ending last rep at **: 5 X-sts and 12 Ldc.

Row 42: Rep row 2: 45 sc.

Row 43: Rep row 7 of Back: 10 Ldc.

Row 44: Rep row 2: 45 sc.

Rows 45–49: Rep rows 5–9: 5 X-sts and 12 Ldc.

Rows 50–52: Rep rows 26–28: 49 sc.

Row 53: Rep row 13: 6 X-sts and 10 Ldc.

Rows 54–56: Rep rows 30–32: 49 sc.

Row 57: Rep row 29: 5 X-sts and 12 Ldc.

Rows 58–60: Rep rows 14–16: 51 sc.

Row 61: Ch 1, turn; sc in first 4 sc, * work X-st over next 3 sts, sk next sc on working row, sc in next sc **, (Ldc in 2nd sc from prev Ldc 3 rows below, sk next sc on working row, sc in next sc) twice; rep from * across, ending last rep at **, sc in last 3 sc: 6 X-sts and 10 Ldc.

Rows 62–64: Rep rows 38–40: 53 sc.

Rows 65: Ch 1, turn; sc in first sc, * work X-st over next 3 sts, sk next sc on working row, sc in next sc **, (Ldc in 2nd sc from prev Ldc 3 rows below, sk next sc on working row, sc in next sc) twice; rep from * across, ending last rep at **: 7 X-sts and 12 Ldc.

Rows 66–68: Rep rows 42–44: 53 sc.

Row 69: Rep row 9 of Back; fasten off: 6 X-sts and 14 Ldc.

Medium and Large Sleeve *(Make 2.)*

Color sequence: *(2 rows MC, 2 rows A) 10 times, (1 row MC, 1 row B, 2 rows A, 1 row B, fasetn off B, 1 row MC, 2 rows A) 3 times, 1 row MC.*

Rows 1–3: Rep rows 1–3 of Small Sleeve.

Row 4: Rep row 6 of Small Sleeve: 31 sc.

Row 5: Rep row 25 of Small Sleeve: 4 X-sts and 6 Ldc.

Row 6: Rep row 6 of Small Sleeve: 33 sc.

Rows 7–21: Rep rows 11–25 of Small Sleeve: 5 X-sts and 8 Ldc.

Rows 22–24: Rep rows 10–12 of Small Sleeve: 41 sc.

Row 25: Rep row 29 of Small Sleeve: 4 X-sts and 10 Ldc.

Rows 26–28: Rep rows 14–16 of Small Sleeve: 43 sc.

Row 29: Rep row 61 of Small Sleeve: 5 X-sts and 8 Ldc.

Rows 30–32: Rep rows 18–20 of Small Sleeve: 45 sc.

Rows 33–53: Rep rows 5–25 of Small Sleeve: 7 X-sts and 12 Ldc.

Rows 54–56: Rep rows 10–12 of Small Sleeve: 57 sc.

Row 57: Rep row 29 of Small Sleeve: 6 X-sts and 14 Ldc.

Rows 58–60: Rep rows 14–16 of Small Sleeve: 59 sc.

Row 61: Rep row 61 of Small Sleeve: 7 X-sts and 12 Ldc.

Rows 62–64: Rep rows 18–20 of Small Sleeve: 61 sc.

Row 65: Rep row 5 of Back; fasten off: 8 X-sts and 14 Ldc.

Extra-large and Extra-extra-large Sleeve *(Make 2.)*

Color sequence: *(2 rows MC, 2 rows A) 9 times, (1 row MC, 1 row B, 2 rows A, 1 row B, fasten off B, 1 row MC, 2 rows A) 3 times, 1 row MC.*

Rows 1–6: Rep rows 1–6 of Medium and Large Sleeve.

Row 7: Rep row 11 of Small Sleeve: 8 Ldc.

Row 8: Rep row 6 of Small Sleeve: 35 sc.

Row 9: Ch 1, turn; sc in first 4 sc, Ldc in 4th sc from beg 3 rows below, * sk next sc on working row, sc in next sc, Ldc in 2nd sc from prev Ldc 3 rows below, sk next sc on working row, sc in next sc **, work X-st over next 3 sts, sk next sc on working row, sc in next sc, Ldc in 2nd sc from prev Ldc 3 rows below; rep from * across, ending last rep at **, sc in last 3 sc: 3 X-sts and 8 Ldc.

Row 10: Rep row 6 of Small Sleeve: 37 sc.

Row 11: Rep row 19 of Small Sleeve: 8 Ldc.

Row 12: Rep row 6 of Small Sleeve: 39 sc.

Row 13: Ch 1, turn; sc in first 2 sc, Ldc in 2nd sc from beg 3 rows below, * sk next sc on working row, sc in next sc, Ldc in 2nd sc from prev Ldc 3 rows below, sk next sc on working row, sc in next sc **, work X-st over next 3 sts, sk next sc on working row, sc in next sc, Ldc in 2nd sc from prev Ldc 3 rows below; rep from * across, ending last rep at **,

(Continued on page 132)

sc in last sc: 4 X-sts and 10 Ldc.

Rows 14–16: Rep rows 6–8 once: 43 sc.

Row 17: Rep row 61 of Small Sleeve: 5 X-sts and 8 Ldc.

Rows 18–20: Rep rows 10–12 once: 47 sc.

Rows 21–27: Rep rows 5–11 once: 12 Ldc.

Rows 28–33: Rep rows 20–25 of Small Sleeve: 55 sc.

Rows 34 and 35: Rep rows 6 and 7 once: 14 Ldc.

Row 36: Rep row 2 of Small Sleeve: 57 sc.

Row 37: Ch 1, turn; sc in first 3 sc, Ldc in 4th sc from beg 3 rows below, * sk next sc on working row, sc in next sc, Ldc in 2nd sc from prev Ldc 3 rows below, sk next sc on working row, sc in next sc **, work X-st over next 3 sts, sk next sc on working row, sc in next sc, Ldc in 2nd sc from prev Ldc 3 rows below; rep from * across, ending last rep at **; sc in last 2 sc: 6 X-sts and 14 Ldc.

Rows 38–40: Rep rows 14–16 of Small Sleeve: 59 sc.

Rows 41–43: Rep rows 17–19 once: 14 Ldc.

Row 44: Rep row 2 of Small Sleeve: 61 sc.

Row 45: Rep row 5 of Back: 8 X-sts and 14 Ldc.

Rows 46–60: Rep rows 6–20 of Small Sleeve: 69 sts.

Row 61: Rep row 9 of Back; fasten off: 8 X-sts and 18 Ldc.

Assembly

With rs facing, whipstitch shoulder seams tog. Mark bottom of Armholes 8¾" {10", 10", 11½", 11½"} from shoulder seams on Front and Back. With rs tog, align top center of 1 Sleeve with shoulder seam and whipstitch Sleeve to Body from marker to marker; rep for rem Sleeve. With rs tog, whipstitch side seams and Sleeve seams tog.

Neck Ribbing

With A and smaller hook, ch 7 loosely.

Work as for Ribbing for 84 {88, 88, 88, 92} rows; fasten off after last row. With rs facing, whipstitch first and last rows tog. With rs tog, whipstitch Neck Ribbing to Body.

Project was stitched by Marge Wild with Wool-ease: Black #153, Denim #114, and Natural Heather #98.

Christmas Stripes

Panels stitched in the brightest colors of the season add holiday cheer to any room.

Materials

Worsted-weight acrylic yarn, approximately:

24 oz. (1,200 yd.) white, MC
30 oz. (1,500 yd.) red, A
24 oz. (1,200 yd.) green, B
Size K crochet hook or size to obtain gauge
Yarn needle

Finished Size

Approximately 58" x 70"

Gauge

In pat, 10 sts and 12 rows = 4"

Gauge Swatch *(Multiple of 4 sts + 2)*

With B, ch 14. Work as for Strip A for 16 rows.

Pattern Stitch

Long double crochet [Ldc]: Yo, insert hook from front to back in st indicated, yo and pull up long lp, (yo and pull through 2 lps) twice.

Note: To change colors, work last yo of prev st with new color, dropping prev color to ws of work. Do not fasten off when changing colors.

Strip A *(Make 4.)*

With B, ch 14 loosely.

Row 1 (rs): Sc in 2nd ch from hook and in ea ch across, change to A in last st: 13 sc.

Row 2 (ws): With A, ch 1, turn; sc in first sc and in ea sc across, change to MC in last st.

Row 3: With MC, ch 1, turn; sc in first sc and in ea st across, change to B in last st.

Row 4: With B, ch 1, turn; sc in first sc, Ldc in 3rd sc from beg 3 rows below, * sk next sc on working row, sc in next sc, Ldc in same sc as prev Ldc 3 rows below [V-st made], sk next sc on working row, sc in next sc **, Ldc in 4th sc from prev Ldc 3 rows below; rep from * across, ending last rep at **, change to A in last st: 3 V-sts.

Row 5: Rep row 2.

Row 6: With MC, ch 1, turn; sc in first 3 sc, Ldc in 5th sc from beg 3 rows below, * sk next sc on working row, sc in next sc, Ldc in same sc as prev Ldc 3 rows below [V-st made], sk next sc on working row, sc in next sc **, Ldc in 4th sc from prev Ldc 3 rows below; rep from * across, ending last rep at **, sc in last 2 sc, change to B in last st: 2 V-sts.

Row 7: With B, ch 1, turn; sc in first sc and in ea st across, change to A in last st.

Row 8: With A, ch 1, turn; sc in first sc, Ldc in 3rd sc from beg 3 rows below, * sk next sc on working row, sc in next sc, Ldc in same sc as prev Ldc 3 rows below [V-st made], sk next sc on working row, sc in next sc **, Ldc in 4th sc from prev Ldc 3 rows below; rep from * across, ending last rep at **, change to MC in last st: 3 V-sts.

Row 9: Rep row 3.

Row 10: With B, ch 1, turn; sc in first 3 sc, Ldc in 5th sc from beg 3 rows below, * sk next sc on working row, sc in next sc, Ldc in same sc as prev Ldc 3 rows below [V-st made], sk next sc on working row, sc in next sc **, Ldc in 4th sc from prev Ldc 3 rows below; rep from * across, ending last rep at **, sc in last 2 sc, change to A in last st: 2 V-sts.

Row 11: Rep row 2.

Row 12: With MC, ch 1, turn; sc in first sc, Ldc in 3rd sc from beg 3 rows below, * sk next sc on working row, sc in next sc, Ldc in same sc as prev Ldc 3 rows below [V-st made], sk next sc on working row, sc in next sc **, Ldc in 4th sc from prev Ldc 3 rows below; rep from * across, ending last rep at **, change to B in last st: 3 V-sts.

Row 13: Rep row 7.

Row 14: With A, ch 1, turn; sc in first 3 sc, Ldc in 5th sc from beg

3 rows below, * sk next sc on working row, sc in next sc, Ldc in same sc as prev Ldc 3 rows below [V-st made], sk next sc on working row, sc in next sc **, Ldc in 4th sc from prev Ldc 3 rows below; rep from * across, ending last rep at **, sc in last 2 sc, change to MC in last st: 2 V-sts.
Rows 15–208: Rep rows 3–14, 16 times, then rep rows 3 and 4 once; fasten off after last row.

Strip B *(Make 1.)*
With MC, ch 30 loosely.
Row 1 (rs): Sc in 2nd ch from hook and in ea ch across: 29 sc.
Row 2 (ws): Ch 1, turn; sc in first sc and in ea sc across.
Row 3: Ch 1, turn; sc in first sc and in ea st across.
Row 4: Ch 1, turn; sc in first 3 sc, Ldc in 5th sc from beg 3 rows below, * sk next sc on working row, sc in next sc, Ldc in same sc as prev Ldc 3 rows below [V-st made], sk next sc on working row, sc in next sc **, Ldc in 4th sc from prev Ldc 3 rows below; rep from * across, ending last rep at **, sc in last 2 sc: 6 V-sts.
Row 5: Rep row 3.
Row 6: Ch 1, turn; sc in first sc, Ldc in 3rd sc from beg 3 rows below, * sk next sc on working row, sc in next sc, Ldc in same sc as prev Ldc 3 rows below [V-st made], sk next sc on working row, sc in next sc **, Ldc in 4th sc from prev Ldc 3 rows below; rep from * across, ending last rep at **: 7 V-sts.
Rows 7–208: Rep rows 3–6, 50 times, then rep rows 3 and 4 once; fasten off after last row.

Strip C *(Make 2.)*
With A, ch 22 loosely.
Row 1 (rs): Sc in 2nd ch from hook and in ea ch across: 21 sc.
Row 2 (ws): Ch 1, turn; sc in first sc and in ea sc across.

Row 3: Ch 1, turn; sc in first sc and in ea st across.
Row 4: Ch 1, turn; sc in first 3 sc, Ldc in 5th sc from beg 3 rows below, * sk next sc on working row, sc in next sc, Ldc in same sc as prev Ldc 3 rows below [V-st made], sk next sc on working row **, sc in next sc, Ldc in 4th sc from prev Ldc 3 rows below; rep from * across, ending last rep at **, sc in last 2 sc: 4 V-sts.
Row 5: Rep row 3.
Row 6: Ch 1, turn; sc in first sc, Ldc in 3rd sc from beg 3 rows below, * sk next sc on working row, sc in next sc, Ldc in same sc as prev Ldc 3 rows below [V-st made], sk next sc on working row, sc in next sc **, Ldc in 4th sc from prev Ldc 3 rows below; rep from * across, ending last rep at **: 5 V-sts.
Rows 7–208: Rep rows 3–6, 50 times, then rep rows 3 and 4 once; fasten off after last row.

Strip D *(Make 2.)*
With B, ch 14 loosely.
Row 1 (rs): Sc in 2nd ch from hook and in ea ch across: 13 sc.
Row 2 (ws): Ch 1, turn; sc in first sc and in ea sc across.
Row 3: Ch 1, turn; sc in first sc and in ea st across.
Row 4: Ch 1, turn; sc in first 3 sc, Ldc in 5th sc from beg 3 rows below, * sk next sc on working row, sc in next sc, Ldc in same sc as prev Ldc 3 rows below [V-st made], sk next sc on working row, sc in next sc **, Ldc in 4th sc from prev Ldc 3 rows below; rep from * across, ending last rep at **, sc in last 2 sc: 2 V-sts.
Row 5: Rep row 3.
Row 6: Ch 1, turn; sc in first sc, Ldc in 3rd sc from beg 3 rows below, * sk next sc on working row, sc in next sc, Ldc in same sc as prev Ldc 3 rows below [V-st made], sk next sc on working row,

sc in next sc **, Ldc in 4th sc from prev Ldc 3 rows below; rep from * across, ending last rep at **: 3 V-sts.
Rows 7–208: Rep rows 3–6, 50 times, then rep rows 3 and 4 once; fasten off after last row.

Assembly
Arrange strips with rs facing in foll sequence: Strip D, Strip A, Strip C, Strip A, Strip B, Strip A, Strip C, Strip A, Strip D. Turn all Strip As upside down. Whipstitch Strips tog.

Border
Rnd 1 (rs): With rs facing, join MC in any corner with sl st, ch 1, * sc evenly across to next corner, 3 sc in corner; rep from * around; join with sl st to beg sc; fasten off.
Rnd 2 (ws): With ws facing, join A in any corner with sl st, ch 1, * sc in ea sc across to corner, 3 sc in corner; rep from * around; join with sl st to beg sc; fasten off.
Rnd 3 (rs): With rs facing and B, rep rnd 2; do not fasten off.
Rnd 4 (rs): With rs facing and B, sl st in same sc and in ea sc around; join with sl st to beg sl st; fasten off.

Project was stitched by Marge Wild with Jamie 4-ply: White #100, Red #113, and Evergreen #130.

Quick and Cozy

Curl up on the coldest nights with an extrathick chenille blanket.
Chunky yarn and a large hook make this afghan grow rapidly.

Materials
Super chunky-weight chenille yarn, approximately:
45 oz. (850 yd.) blue, MC
40 oz. (755 yd.) cream, CC
Size N crochet hook or size to obtain gauge

Finished Size
Approximately 54" x 66"

Gauge
In pat, 8 sts and 8½ rows = 5"

Gauge Swatch *(Multiple of 5 sts + 4)*
With MC, ch 19. Work in pat for 10 rows.

Pattern Stitch
Long double crochet [Ldc]: Yo, insert hook from front to back in st indicated, yo and pull up long lp, (yo and pull through 2 lps) twice.

Note: To change colors, work last yo of prev st with new color, dropping prev color to ws of work. Do not fasten off when changing colors.

With MC, ch 84 loosely.
Row 1 (ws): Sc in 2nd ch from hook and in ea ch across, change to CC in last st: 83 sc.
Row 2 (rs): With CC, ch 1, turn; sc in first sc and in ea sc across.
Row 3: Ch 1, turn; sc in first sc and in ea st across, change to MC in last st.
Row 4: With MC, ch 1, turn; sc in first sc, Ldc in 4th sc from beg 3 rows below [slant-st made],

* sk next sc on working row, sc in next sc, Ldc in same sc as prev Ldc, sk next sc on working row, sc in next 2 sc **, Ldc in 5th sc from prev Ldc [slant-st made]; rep from * across, ending last rep at **, sc in last 2 sc: 16 Ldc and 16 slant-sts.
Row 5: Ch 1, turn; sc in first sc and in ea st across, change to CC in last st.
Row 6: With CC, ch 1, turn; sc in first 4 sc, Ldc in 5th sc from beg 3 rows below, * sk next sc on working row, sc in next sc, Ldc in same sc as prev Ldc 3 rows below [slant-st made], sk next sc on working row **, sc in next 2 sc, Ldc in 5th sc from prev Ldc 3 rows below; rep from * across, ending last rep at **, sc in last sc: 16 Ldc and 16 slant-sts.

Rows 7–108: Rep rows 3–6, 25 times, then rep rows 3 and 4 once; do not turn after last row; fasten off CC; do not fasten off MC.

Border
Rnd 1 (rs): With rs facing and MC, ch 1, 3sc in last st, sc evenly across to next corner, 3 sc in corner, sc in ea ch across to next corner, 3 sc in corner, sc evenly across to next corner, 3 sc in corner, sc in ea st across to next corner; join with sl st to beg sc.
Rnd 2 (ws): Turn; sl st in same sc and in ea sc around; join with sl st to beg sl st; fasten off.

Project was stitched by Joann Moss with Chenille Thick & Quick: Dusty Blue #108 and Antique White #098.

General Directions

Crochet Abbreviations

beg	begin(ning)	ft lp(s)	front loop(s)	st(s)	stitch(es)
bet	between	grp(s)	group(s)	tch	turning chain
bk lp(s)	back loop(s)	hdc	half double crochet	tog	together
ch	chain(s)	inc	increas(es) (ed) (ing)	tr	triple crochet
ch-	refers to chain	lp(s)	loop(s)	yo	yarn over
	previously made	pat(s)	pattern(s)		
cl	cluster(s)	prev	previous		
cont	continu(e) (ing)	rem	remain(s) (ing)		
dc	double crochet	rep	repeat(s)		
dec	decreas(es) (ed) (ing)	rnd(s)	round(s)		
dtr	double triple crochet	sc	single crochet		
ea	each	sk	skip(ped)		
est	established	sl st	slip stitch		
foll	follow(s) (ing)	sp(s)	space(s)		

Repeat whatever follows * as indicated. "Rep from * 3 times more" means to work 4 times in all.

Work directions given in parentheses ( ) and brackets [ ] the number of times specified or in the place specified.

Aluminum Crochet Hook Sizes

U.S.	Size	Metric	Canada/U.K.	U.S.	Size	Metric	Canada/U.K.
B	(1)	2.25	13	H	(8)	5.00	6
C	(2)	2.75		I	(9)	5.50	5
D	(3)	3.25	10	J	(10)	6.00	4
E	(4)	3.50	9	K	(10½)	6.50	3
F	(5)	4.00		N		10.00	000
G	(6)	4.25	8				

Metric Conversion
Common Measures

⅛" = 3 mm	5" = 12.7 cm	⅛ yard = 0.11 m
¼" = 6 mm	6" = 15.2 cm	¼ yard = 0.23 m
⅜" = 9 mm	7" = 17.8 cm	⅓ yard = 0.3 m
½" = 1.3 cm	8" = 20.3 cm	⅜ yard = 0.34 m
⅝" = 1.6 cm	9" = 22.9 cm	½ yard = 0.46 m
¾" = 1.9 cm	10" = 25.4 cm	⅝ yard = 0.57 m
⅞" = 2.2 cm	11" = 27.9 cm	⅔ yard = 0.61 m
1" = 2.5 cm	12" = 30.5 cm	¾ yard = 0.69 m
2" = 5.1 cm	36" = 91.5 cm	⅞ yard = 0.8 m
3" = 7.6 cm	45" = 114.3 cm	1 yard = 0.91 m
4" = 10.2 cm	60" = 152.4 cm	

Note to Left-Handed Crocheters

Since instructions for crocheted projects most often appear with right-handed instructions only, it may be worth your while to learn right-handed crochet techniques. Since the work is shared between the hands in crochet, it may be surprisingly easy for you to make use of the accompanying diagrams. If working in this way is not comfortable, use a mirror to reverse the diagrams or reverse them on a photocopier.

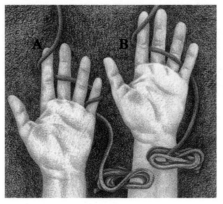

Holding the Hook

Hold the hook as you would a piece of chalk **(A)** or a pencil **(B)**. If your hook has a finger rest, position your thumb and opposing finger there for extra control.

Holding the Yarn

Weave the yarn through the fingers of your left hand. Some people like to wrap the yarn around the little finger for extra control **(A)**; some do not **(B)**. In either case, the forefinger plays the most important role in regulating tension as yarn is fed into the work.

Working Together

Once work has begun, the thumb and the middle finger of the left hand come into play, pressing together to hold the stitches just made.

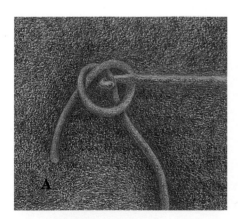

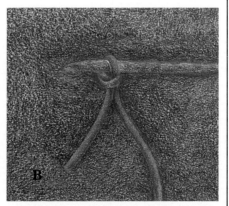

Gauge

Before beginning a project, work a 4"-square gauge swatch, using the recommended size hook. Count and compare the number of stitches per inch in the swatch with the designer's gauge. If you have fewer stitches in your swatch, try a smaller hook; if you have more stitches, try a larger hook.

Slip Knot

A. Loop the yarn around and let the loose end of the yarn fall behind the loop to form a pretzel shape as shown. Insert the hook.

B. Pull both ends to close the knot.

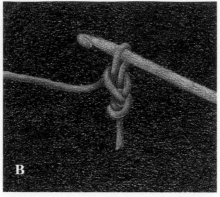

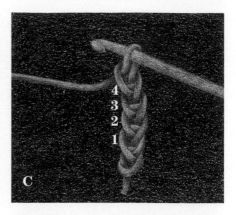

Chain Stitch

A. Place slip knot on hook. With thumb and middle finger of left hand holding yarn end, wrap yarn up and over hook (from back to front). This movement is called "yarn over (yo)" and is basic to every crochet stitch.

B. Use hook to pull yarn through loop (lp) already on hook. Combination of yo and pulling yarn through lp makes 1 chain stitch (ch).

C. Repeat A and B until ch is desired length. Try to keep movements even and relaxed and all ch stitches (sts) same size. Hold ch near working area to keep it from twisting. Count sts as shown in diagram. (Do not count lp on hook or slip knot.)

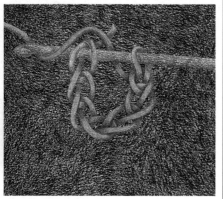

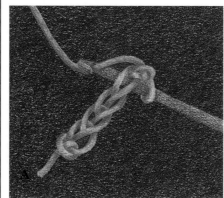

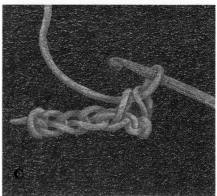

Slip Stitch

Here slip stitch (sl st) is used to join ring. Taking care not to twist chain, insert hook into first ch made, yo and pull through ch and lp on hook (sl st made). Sl st can also be used to join finished pieces or to move across groups of sts without adding height to work.

Single Crochet

A. Insert hook under top 2 lps of 2nd ch from hook and yo. (Always work sts through top 2 lps unless directions specify otherwise.)
B. Yo and pull yarn through ch (2 lps on hook).
C. Yo and pull yarn through 2 lps on hook (1 sc made).

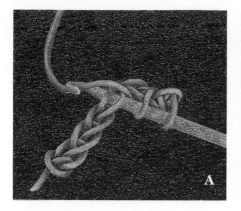
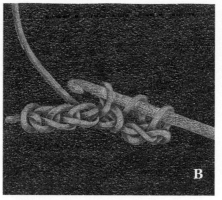
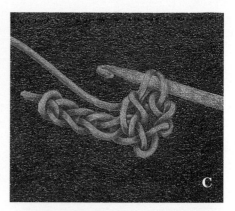

Double Crochet

A. Yo, insert hook into 4th ch from hook, and yo.
B. Yo and pull yarn through ch (3 lps on hook).

C. Yo and pull through 2 lps on hook (2 lps remaining).
D. Yo and pull through 2 remaining (rem) lps (1 dc made).

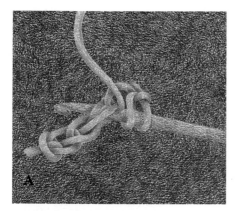
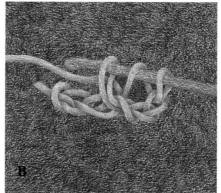
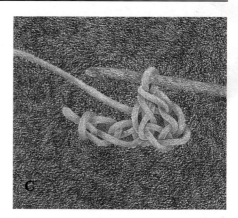

Half Double Crochet

A. Yo and insert hook into 3rd ch from hook.

B. Yo and pull through ch (3 lps on hook).

C. Yo and pull yarn through all 3 lps on hook (1 hdc made).

Triple Crochet

A. Yo twice, insert hook into 5th ch from hook. Yo and pull through ch (4 lps on hook).
B. Yo and pull through 2 lps on hook (3 lps rem). Yo and pull through 2 lps on hook (2 lps rem). Yo and pull through 2 lps on hook (1 tr made).

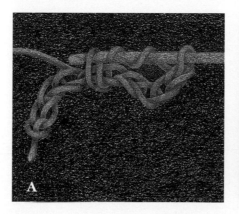
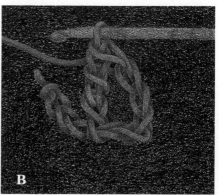

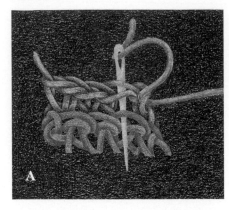

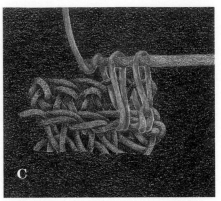

Assembly

To assemble crocheted pieces, use a large-eyed yarn needle to whipstitch **(A)** or a crochet hook to slip stitch **(B)** the pieces together. Pieces can also be joined using single crochet stitches **(C)**, but this makes a heavier seam.

When making squares or other pieces to be stitched together, leave a 20" tail of yarn when fastening off. This yarn tail can then be used to stitch the pieces together, with all stitches and rows of the squares or the strips aligned and running in the same direction.

Joining Yarn

To change colors or to begin a new skein of yarn at the end of a row, work the last yarn over for the last stitch of the previous row with the new yarn.

Fastening Off

Cut the yarn, leaving a 6" tail. Yarn over and pull the tail through the last loop on the hook. Thread the tail into a large-eyed yarn needle and weave it carefully into the back of the work.

Metric Math

When you know:	Multiply by:	To find:	When you know:	Multiply by:	To find:
inches (")	25	millimeters (mm)	millimeters (mm)	0.039	inches (")
inches (")	2.5	centimeters (cm)	centimeters (cm)	0.39	inches (")
inches (")	0.025	meters (m)	meters (m)	39	inches (")
yards (yd.)	0.9	meters (m)	meters (m)	1.093	yards (yd.)
ounces (oz.)	28.35	grams (g)	grams (g)	0.035	ounces (oz.)

Front Post dc (FPdc)

A. Yo and insert hook from front to back around post of st on previous row.
B. Complete dc st as usual.
(Back post dc [BPdc] is worked in same manner, except you insert hook from back to front around post.)

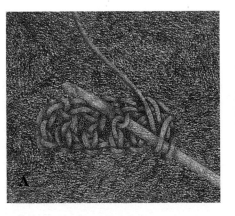

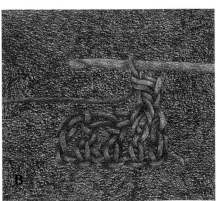

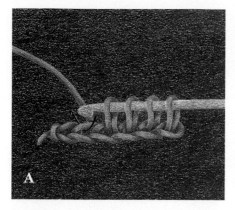

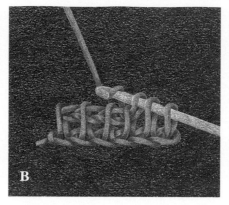

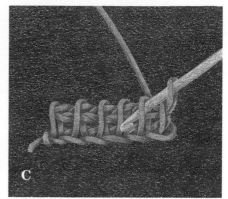

Afghan Stitch

A. *Row 1: Step 1:* Keeping all lps on hook, pull up lp through top lp only in 2nd ch from hook and in ea ch across = same number of lps and chs. Do not turn.
B. *Step 2:* Yo and pull through first lp on hook, * yo and pull through 2 lps on hook, rep from * across (1 lp rem on hook for first lp of next row). Do not turn.
C. *Row 2: Step 1:* Keeping all lps on hook, pull up lp from under 2nd vertical bar, * pull up lp from under next vertical bar, rep from * across. Do not turn. *Step 2:* Rep step 2 of row 1.

Rep both steps of row 2 for required number of rows. Fasten off after last row by working sl st in ea bar across.

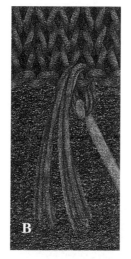

Fringe

To make a simple fringe, cut the required number of yarn lengths as specified in the directions. Insert the hook through 1 stitch at the edge of the afghan and fold the yarn lengths in half over the hook **(A)**. Pull the folded yarn partway through the stitch to form a loop **(B)**. Pull the yarn ends through the loop **(C)** and pull tight **(D)**.

Tassel

Wrap the yarn around a piece of cardboard as specified in the directions. At 1 end, slip a 5" yarn length under the loops and knot tightly. Cut the loops at other end **(A)**. Loop and tightly wrap a 36" yarn length around the tassel **(B)**. Secure the yarn ends and tuck them into the tassel.

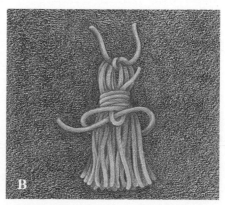

Lion Brand® Yarns

Al•Pa•Ka (Article #740)
Worsted-weight yarn
30% alpaka, 30% wool,
40% acrylic
1¾ oz. (107 yd.) balls

Chenille Sensations
(Article #730)
Worsted-weight yarn
100% Monsanto acrylic
1.4 oz. (87 yd.) skeins

Chenille Thick & Quick
(Article #950)
Chunky-weight yarn
91% acrylic, 9% rayon
5 oz. (94 yd.) skeins

Fishermen's Wool (Article #150)
Worsted-weight yarn
100% wool
8 oz. (465 yd.) skeins

Homespun (Article #790)
Chunky-weight yarn
98% acrylic, 2% polyester
6 oz. (185 yd.) skeins

Imagine (Article #780)
Worsted-weight yarn
80% acrylic, 20% mohair
Solids: 2½ oz. (222 yd.) balls
Multicolors: 2 oz. (179 yd.) balls

Jamie® Baby (Article #870)
Sportweight yarn
100% Monsanto acrylic with
Bounce-Back® fibers
Solids: 1¾ oz. (196 yd.) skeins
Multicolors: 1½ oz. (170 yd.) skeins

Jamie 4 Ply (Article #810)
Worsted-weight yarn
100% Monsanto acrylic with
Bounce-Back® fibers
Solids: 6 oz. (300 yd.) skeins

Jamie® Pompadour
(Article #890)
Sportweight yarn
85% Monsanto acrylic with
Bounce-Back® fibers,
15% rayon wrap
Solids: 1¾ oz. (196 yd.) skeins

Jiffy® (Article #450)
Chunky-weight brushed acrylic
yarn
100% Monsanto acrylic with
Bounce-Back® fibers
Solids: 3 oz. (135 yd.) balls
Multicolors: 2½ oz. (115 yd.) balls

Kitchen Cotton (Article #760)
Worsted-weight yarn
100% cotton
Solids: 5 oz. (236 yd.) balls
Multicolors: 4 oz. (189 yd.) balls

Wool-Ease® (Article #620)
Worsted-weight yarn
Solids and heathers: 80% acrylic,
20% wool
Multicolors: 78% acrylic, 19% wool,
3% polyester
Sprinkles: 86% acrylic, 10% wool,
4% viscose
Frosts: 70% acrylic, 20% wool,
10% polyamide
Solids, heathers, and sprinkles:
3 oz. (197 yd.) balls
Multicolors and frosts: 2½ oz.
(162 yd.) balls

Wool-Ease Thick & Quick
(Article #640)
Chunky-weight yarn
80% acrylic, 20% wool
6 oz. (108 yd.) skeins

Ordering Information
Lion Brand Yarn is widely available
in retail stores across the country.
If you are unable to find Lion
Brand Yarn locally, you may order
it by calling 1-800-258-9276 (YARN).

Special Thanks
Alice Cox
Deborah Hastings
Heather Lettow
Beth McCulley
Suzanne Pizzitola
Barbara Randle
Fay Shannon
Kay Worley

Lily Chin is a New York City
native who began crocheting at
age 8. She started her design
career by selling doilies and
ponchos to teachers and security
guards in junior high school
during the mid-seventies. Now,
Lily is a top designer whose
designs are featured in numerous
crochet magazines and books.

As a young crocheter, Lily has
been cited in several newspapers
across the U.S., including the
*New York Times, Washington
Post, USA Today, Newsday,
Chicago Tribune,* and the *New
York Daily News,* for dispelling
the "granny" image of crochet.
Lily advocates teaching this
traditional craft to anyone who
desires to learn, young or old.

Lily has developed prototypes
for large stores, such as The
Gap, and for couture designers,
such as Isaac Mizrahi. Her work
has appeared on stars and super-
models, including Vanna White,
Racquel Welch, Cindy Crawford,
and Naomi Campbell.

Lily is a member of the
Crochet Guild of America and
conducts workshops, lectures,
and seminars on crochet
throughout the U.S. and Canada.